FAVERSHAM AT WORK

PEOPLE AND INDUSTRIES THROUGH THE YEARS

ROBERT TURCAN

AMBERLEY

ACKNOWLEDGEMENTS

Thanks goes to Keith Chisman for supplying imagery. Appreciation is sincerely given to Tracy Fordyce for her invaluable computer wizardry. Much gratitude is due to Paul Whalen for facilitating aerial shots from his aeroplane. My beloved Jocelyn's support has been infallible. Last but not least I would like to mark the collaboration and help of Marcus Pennington, who edited this volume.

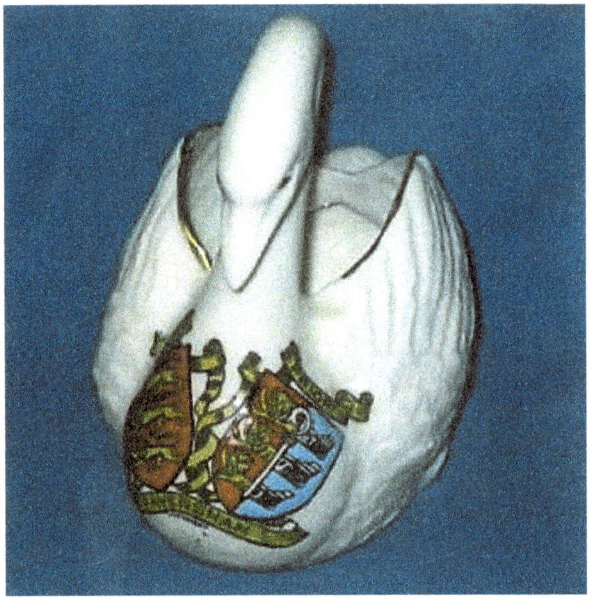

Faversham's motto: 'Market Town of Kings'.

First published 2017

Amberley Publishing
The Hill, Stroud
Gloucestershire, GL5 4EP

www.amberley-books.com

ISBN 978 1 4456 6890 1 (print)
ISBN 978 1 4456 6891 8 (ebook)

British Library Cataloguing in Publication Data. A catalogue record for this book is available from the British Library.

Origination by Amberley Publishing.
Printed in the UK.

CONTENTS

INTRODUCTION

From its very name meaning village of metalworkers Faversham appears to have been a busy, purposeful place. Early settlers came here in prehistoric times as, to quote Igglesden in his *Saunters Through Kent*, it was 'a cosy place with easily cultivated soils'. Presently this town has a population of around 19,000. It is placed between the rural charms of North Downland and austere beauty of Swale wetlands.

For such a small town Faversham has had a disproportionate influence on this country. It was in fact the cradle of our explosive industry. Brick making heritage is yet another major distinction. Indeed much of Victorian metropolitan expansion was built using the famous yellow stock bricks sent in millions from Faversham Creek on sailing barges. Boat building has been significant at various times, but this town will always be primarily associated with its breweries. In particular Shepherd Neame, the country's oldest, still has its headquarters at the core of town in Court Street.

Excellent conditions for farming prevail with fertile soils and a mild climate. The possibility of being able to produce most crops means high-value ones such as fruit and hops are often grown. Well-tended orchards and hop gardens adorn the countryside. The national fruit collection is based at Brogdale and has become renowned worldwide.

Within the town's precincts there are over 500 listed buildings. Tourism is becoming increasingly important, aided by a vibrant retail scene. Lots of interesting specialist shops thrive. They surround Faversham's colourful market – aged over 900 years and held three days per week.

Unique and interesting firms like South Eastern Coachworks have set up here and become exemplary employers, offering good training opportunities. Other larger, more long-standing companies like BMM Weston also make a significant contribution to local prosperity.

With Faversham's location near to the M2 motorway and closeness to London and Dover, it is a good place to be for distribution companies such as Gist, who are contracted to supply haulage services to Marks & Spencer. Warehousing and storage enterprises such as East Kent Storage (EKS) benefit from similar factors.

However, Faversham Creek has for many centuries been its most important transport link. Its seamen defended the realm in medieval and Tudor times. Commercially, the port was once England's largest exporter of wool, and grain and oysters were other major cargoes. Its heyday was the Victorian age when scores of Thames sailing barges conveyed bulk loads of gunpowder, bricks and cement. This mercantile marine activity has all but disappeared. In its place pleasure boating has taken over these inland waterways. Skilled craftsmen still work along the creek side, but generally on smaller vessels than before.

Apart from Faversham's exulted agricultural reputation, its main industries have been summarised by the alliteration 'the four B's': Bangs (explosives), Bricks, Boats and Brewing. This, of course, is an oversimplification as there are a myriad of other people at work in, for example, antique shops, cafés and public services. Last but not least voluntary workers in this town deserve a special mention for their dedication in raising money through charity shops and their proven ability to conserve the special character of Faversham – known as the 'Kings Little Place'.

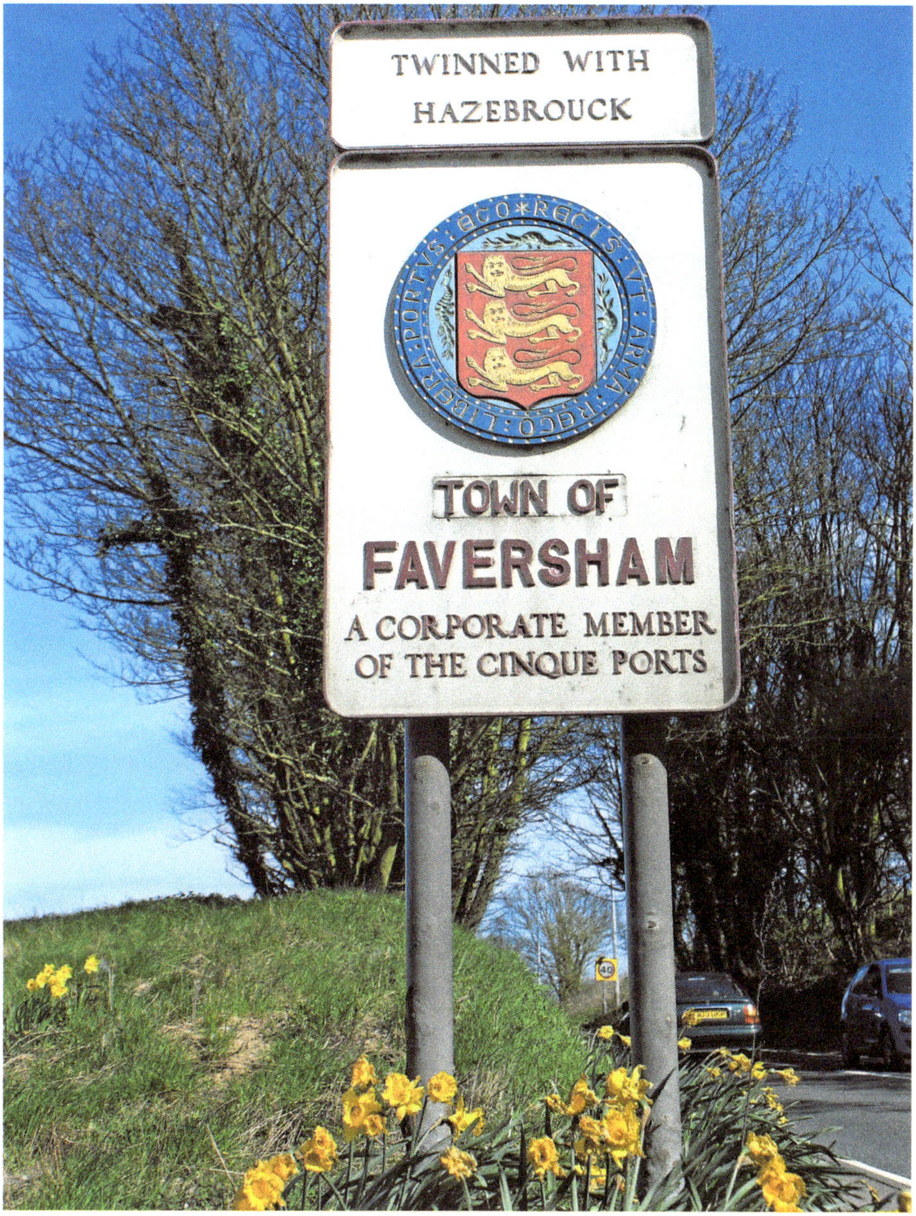

Greeting road sign at Judd's Hill.

EXPLOSIVE INDUSTRY

Faversham is uniquely known for being the cradle of the UK explosive industry. It all began around 1560 in the St Anne's area of the town and was possibly instigated by investment from Faversham Abbey. This establishment had a powerful economic influence over its surroundings and would have been eager to buy into promising new enterprises.

Regardless of who or how this industry began, there were a number of natural elements in its favour. Principally a stream flowed north through Ospringe (a nearby parish straddling the main London to Dover road whose name derives from a bridge crossing a river). This was dammed in places for watermills to provide power for crushing and mixing plant that incorporated the three ingredients of gunpowder. One of these essentials was charcoal made locally from alders grown on the close by flatlands. Sulphur and saltpetre were imported by sea and conveyed from docks upstream.

Strategically Faversham was not only an excellent place for manufacture but also a good place for its markets. Transport was convenient to London magazines or to the Continent where frequent warfare created strong demand.

Early works were small and grouped around the London Road at the head of the stream. Towards the beginning of the eighteenth century, these had amalgamated into a single factory known as Home Works. Around this time the British government's expansive foreign and defence policies required improved armaments. The supply of gunpowder they bought from private sources was of poor quality, and so they decided the most expedient action would be to take over by nationalising the Home Works. Public expenditure was used to upgrade machinery while from thenceforth it was called Chart Gunpowder Mill.

Today the picturesque millpond that powered some of the mills remains along with some of the many narrow canals that linked various stages of production with transport punts. Fortunately, the residents of Faversham are acutely aware of their heritage and have a good record of preserving it. They have restored and protected the remains of Chart Mill, which at times is open to the public. It was saved from developers in 1960s while later in 1980s Mill Pond and its adjacent land was acquired by Swale Borough Council.

A second gunpowder works was established in the late seventeenth century by Huguenot asylum seekers a mile or so west of Chart Mills. Similar natural features prevailed here. In particular another stream offering power and transport prospects. Its link to the sea via Oare Creek was also a vital export connection. Although this factory was called Oare Works, it was something of a misnomer because it was actually in the parish of Davington. One of its best

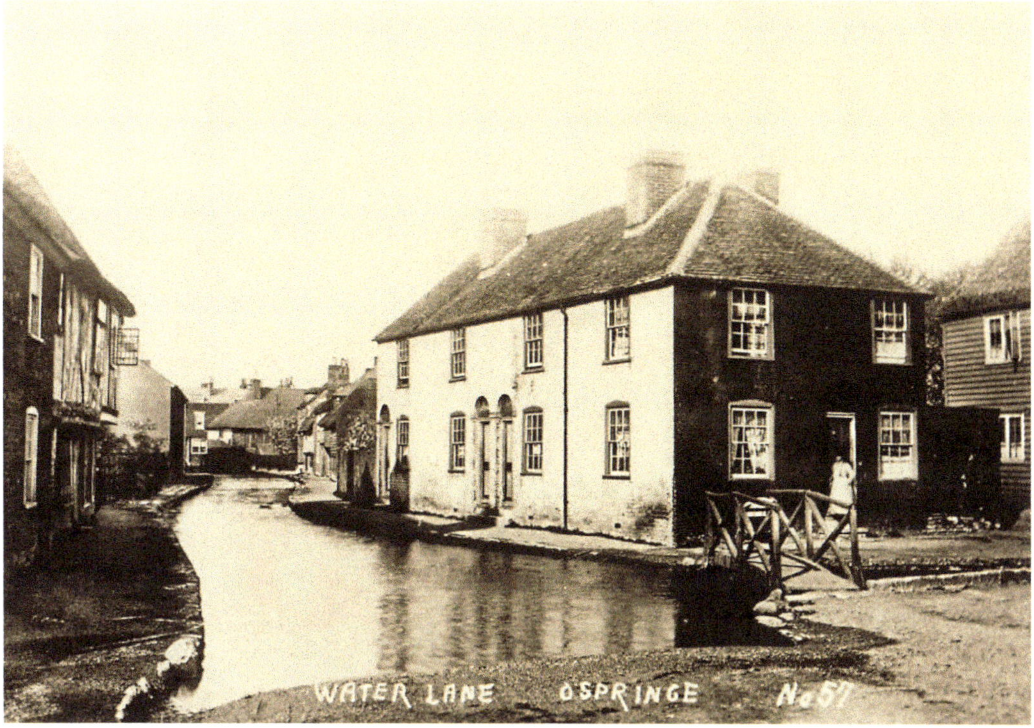

Water Lane, Ospringe, looking north.

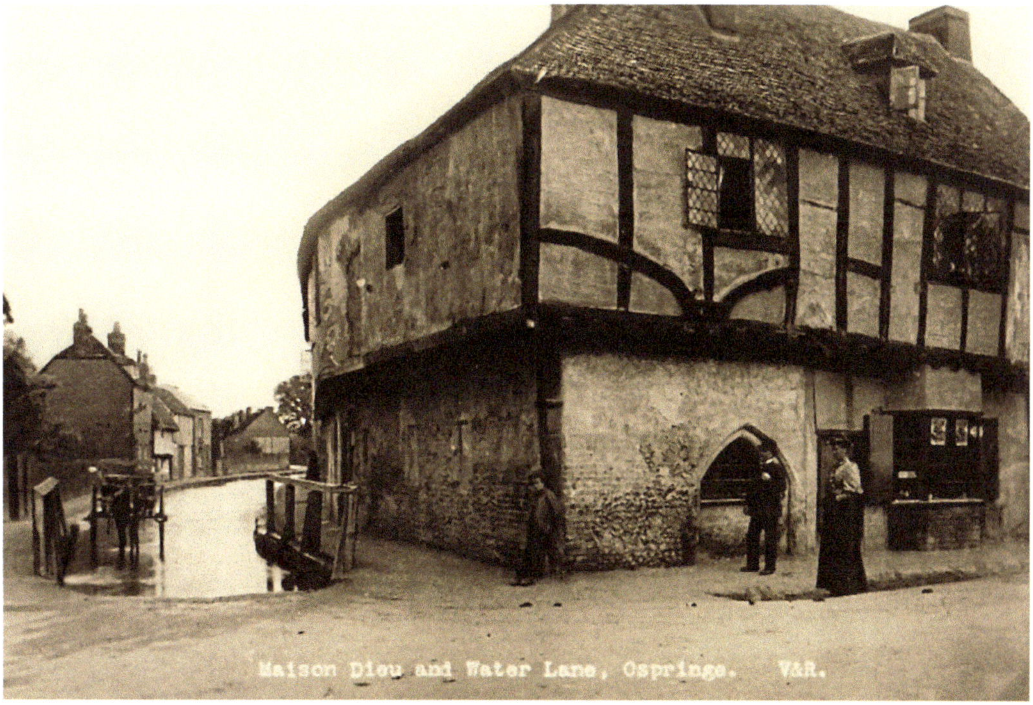

Water Lane, Ospringe, looking south.

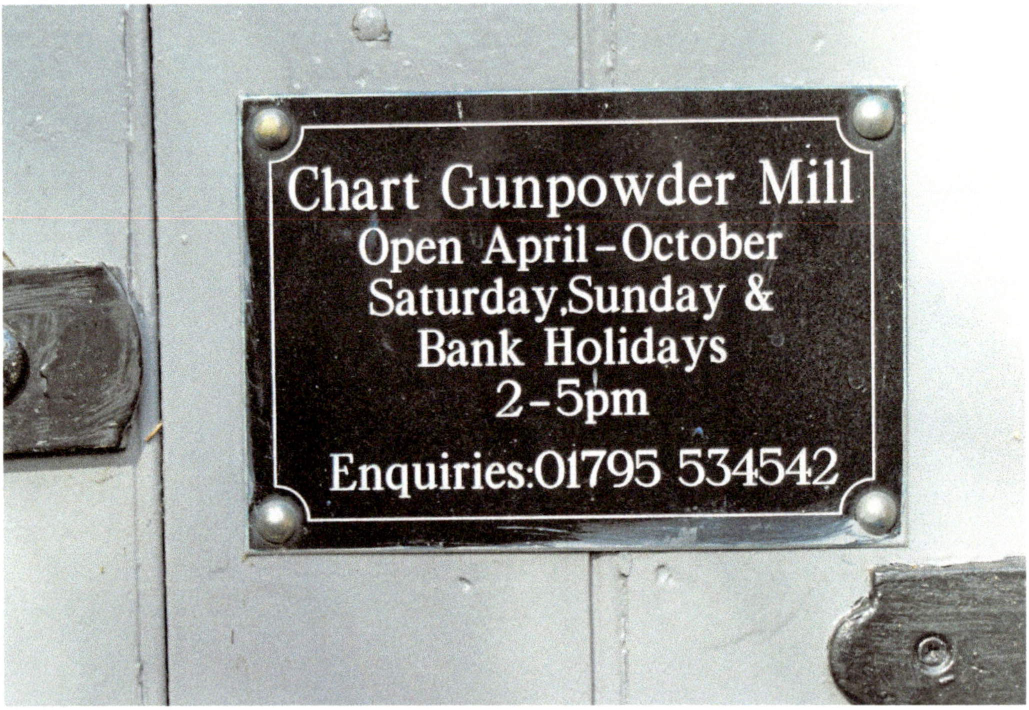

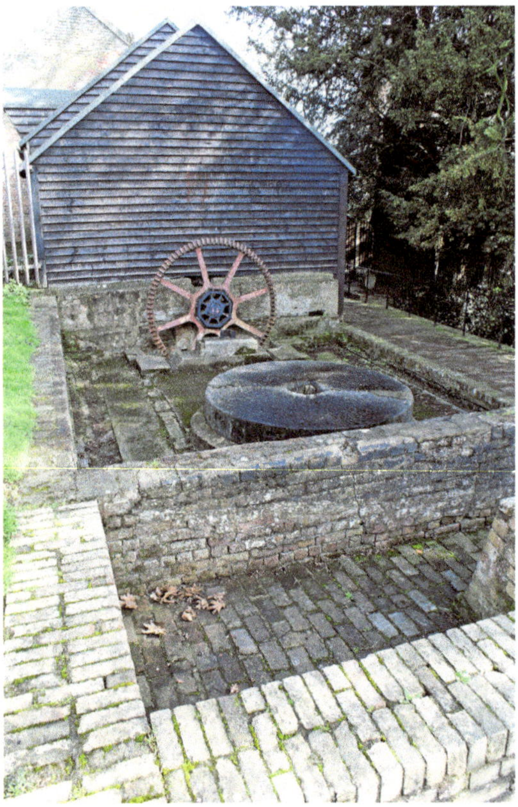

Above: Noticeboard at Chart Gunpowder Mills.

Left: Remaining gearwheel and building foundations.

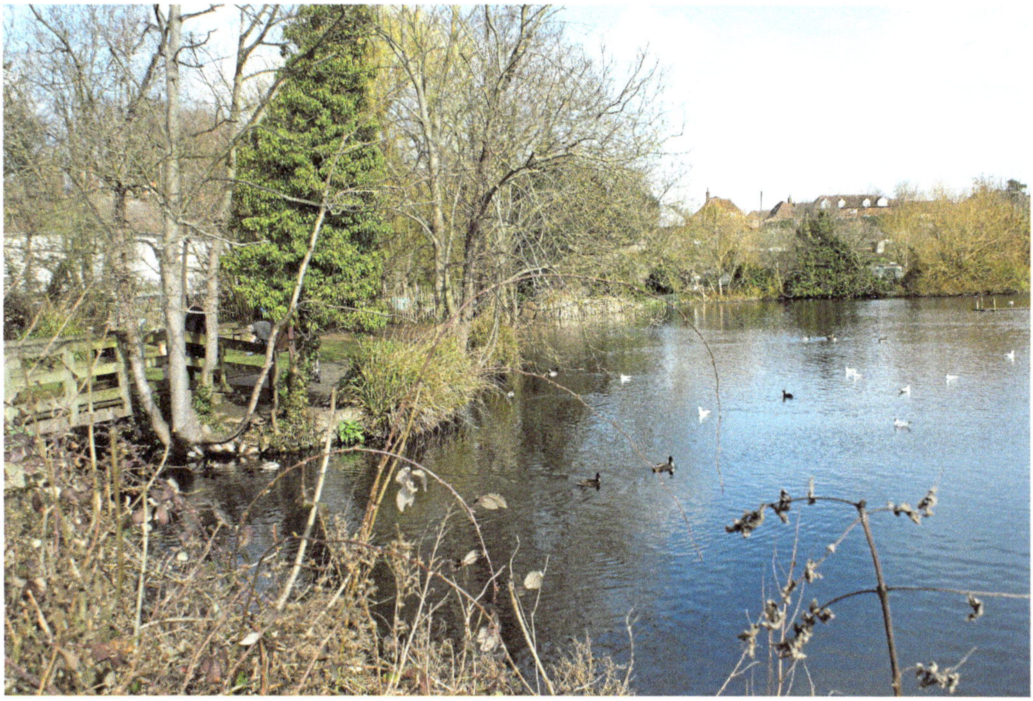

Mill Pond, Faversham.

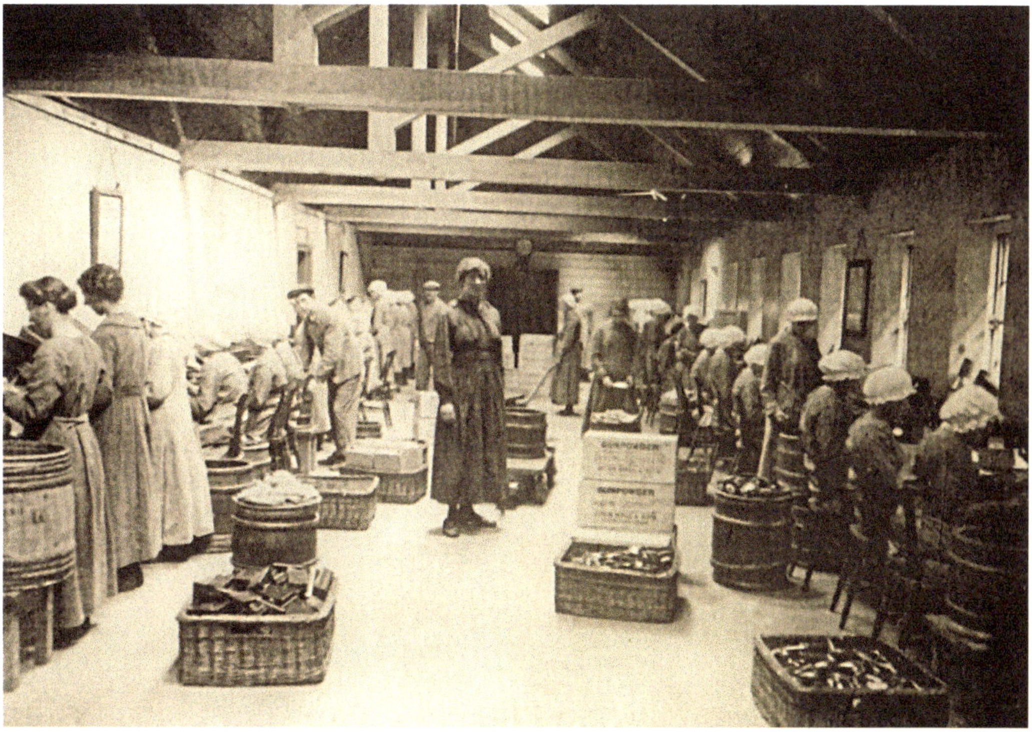

Gunpowder factory workers.

customers was the British East India Company. Perhaps without these supplies Britain could never have conquered and ruled the vast Indian sub-continent.

Apart from military applications, technology associated with gunpowder has had profound civil engineering implications. The progress and pace of the Industrial Revolution was enhanced by blasting routes for canals and railways.

Ironically, sites of gunpowder manufacture are often scenic because shelter belts of trees to shield accidents between buildings were planted and waterways are common features. The Oare Works has become an attractive visitor destination with lovely walkways and interesting relics of its past glory.

Reflecting Britain's growing international significance, in 1787 its government built a third factory nearer the coast at Marsh Works. Although Faversham is a small Kentish town, it has many disproportionately large claims to have featured prominently in history. Not the least of these is the contribution that victories in the Napoleonic battles of Trafalgar and Waterloo were won with gunpowder manufactured there.

After these hostilities the British government gradually returned this industry to private business management. At Marsh Works, a new type of high explosive called guncotton was first made in 1847. Sadly, due to inadequate knowledge and skills, an explosion occurred killing eighteen workers. As a result production ceased. It did, however, resume in 1873. A new enterprise was set up called the Cotton Powder Co. It based its factory at Uplees, which was further distant from the town centre on remote marshland adjoining the sea at Swale River. This proved an ideal spot because raw materials – cotton waste and sulphuric and nitric acids – could be easily landed and finished products similarly dispatched.

Buoyant demand led to rapid growth. Furthermore, executives readily responded to new inventions. A sister company was established to the west where shells and bombs were filled.

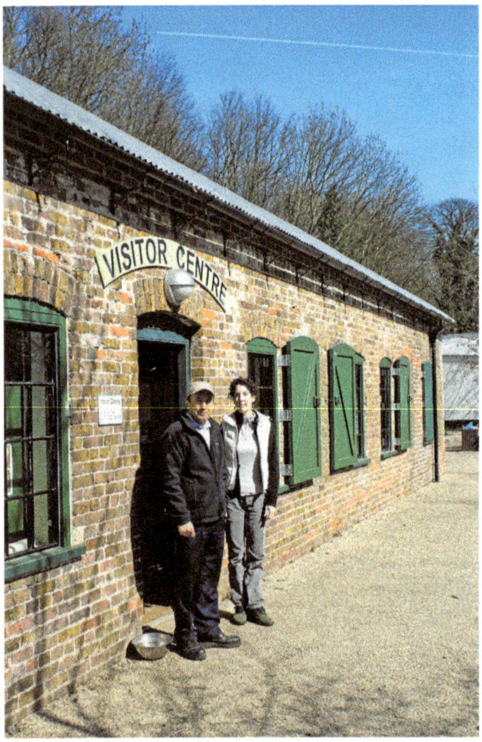

Oare gunpowder factory Visitor Centre.

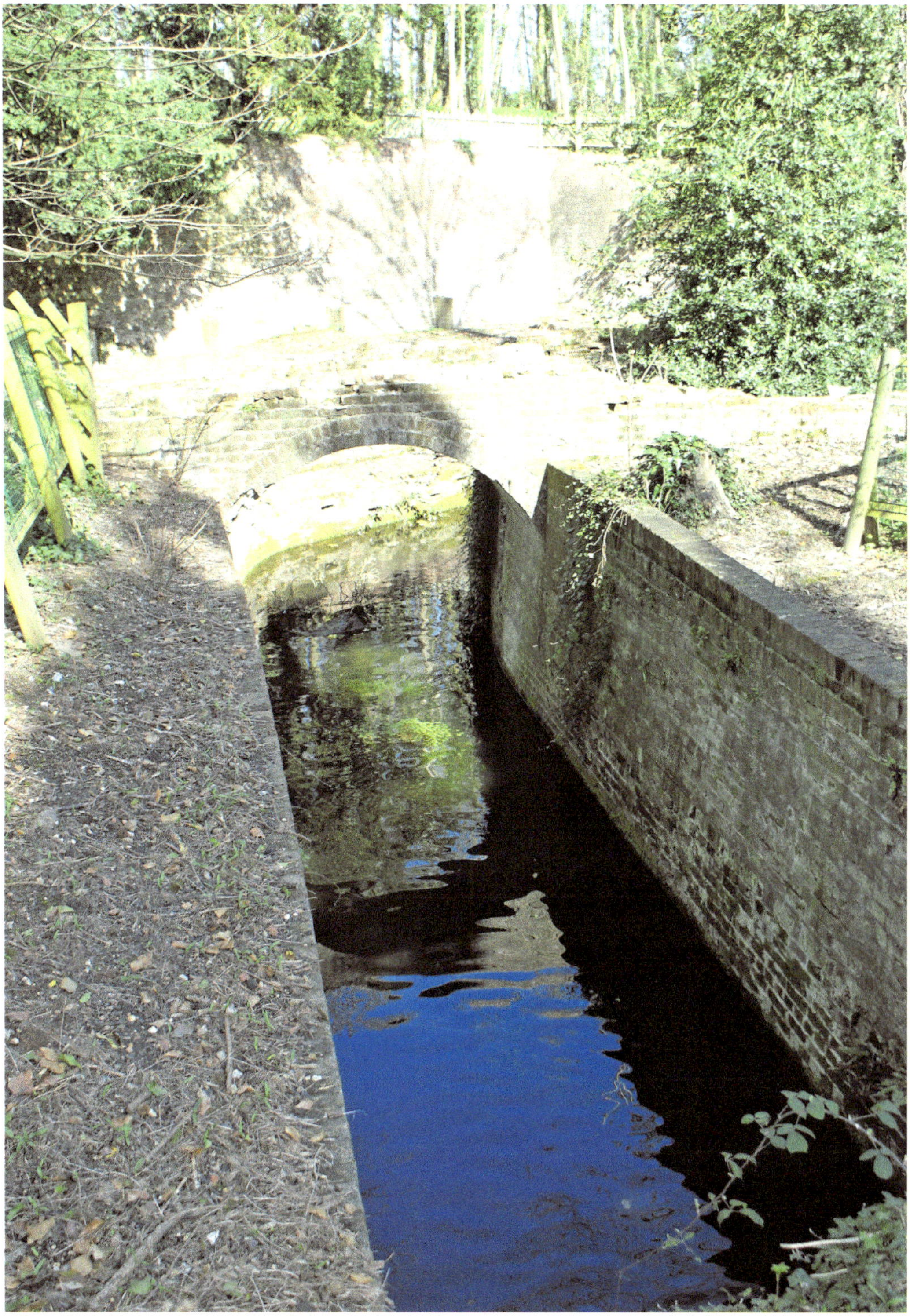

Canal channelling stream.

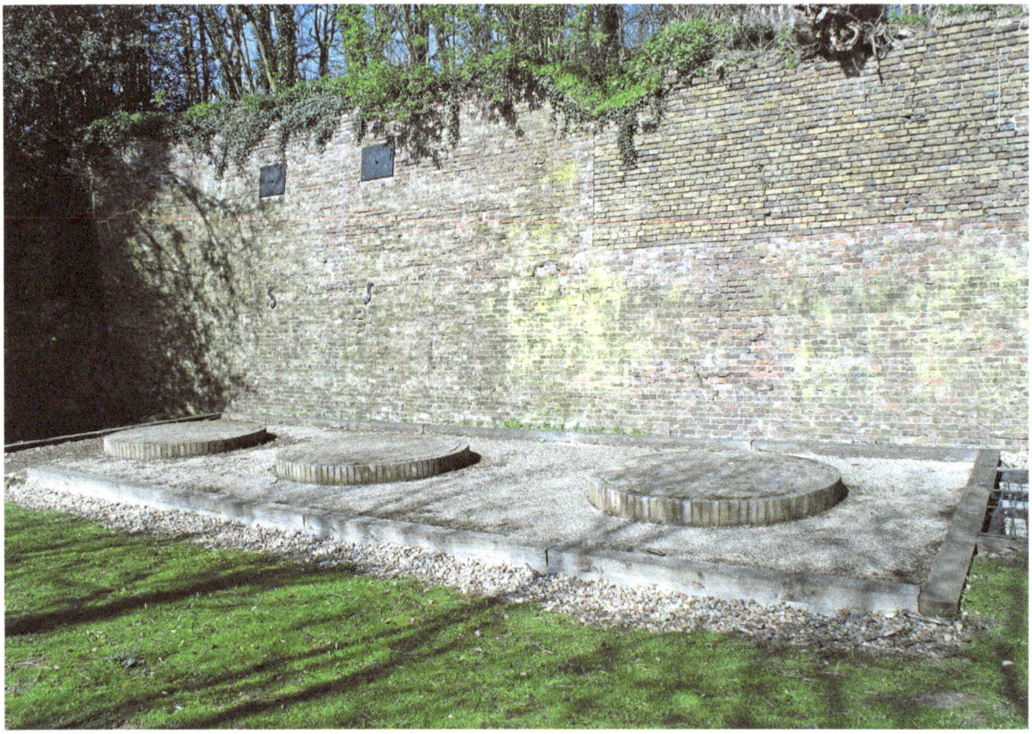

Foundations for grinding and mixing wheels, Oare gunpowder works.

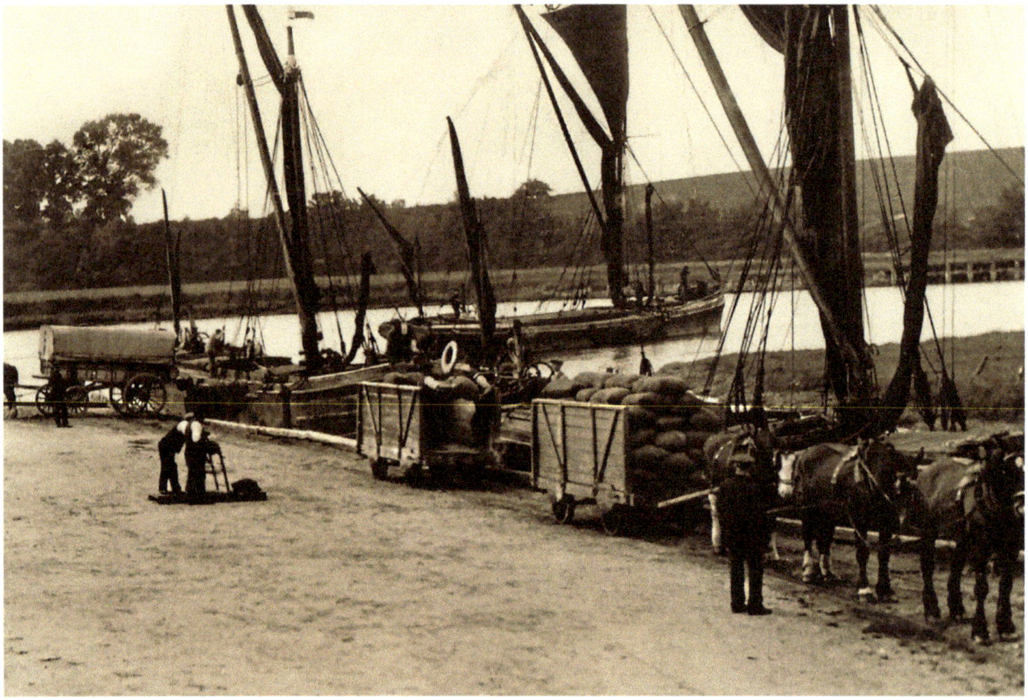

Loading gunpowder onto sailing barges.

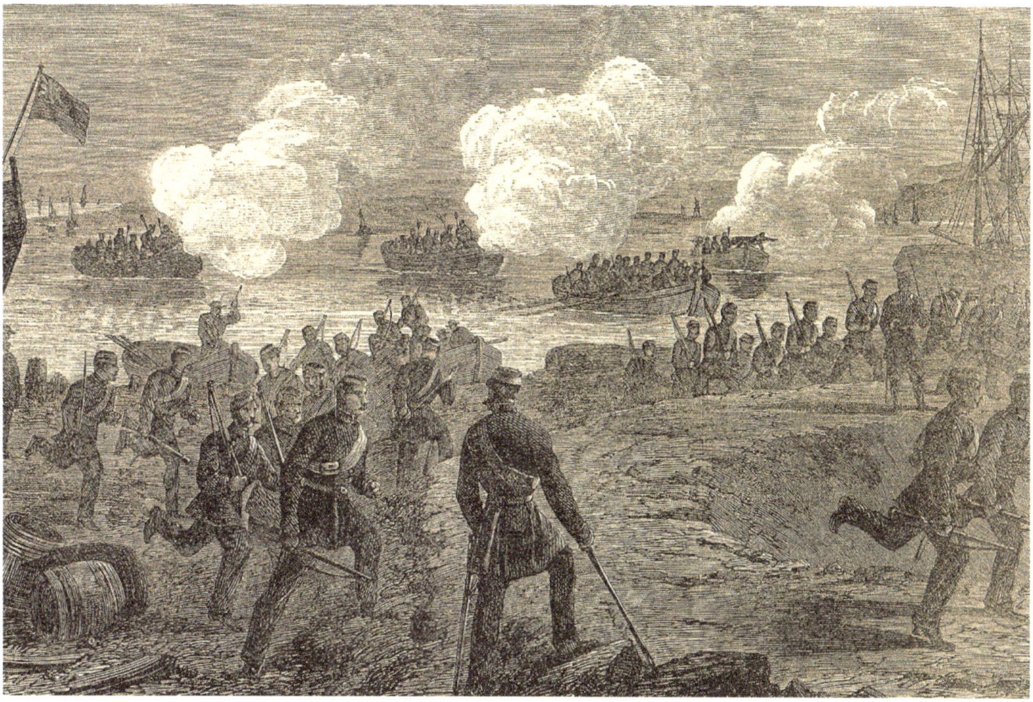

Mock battle of local militia.

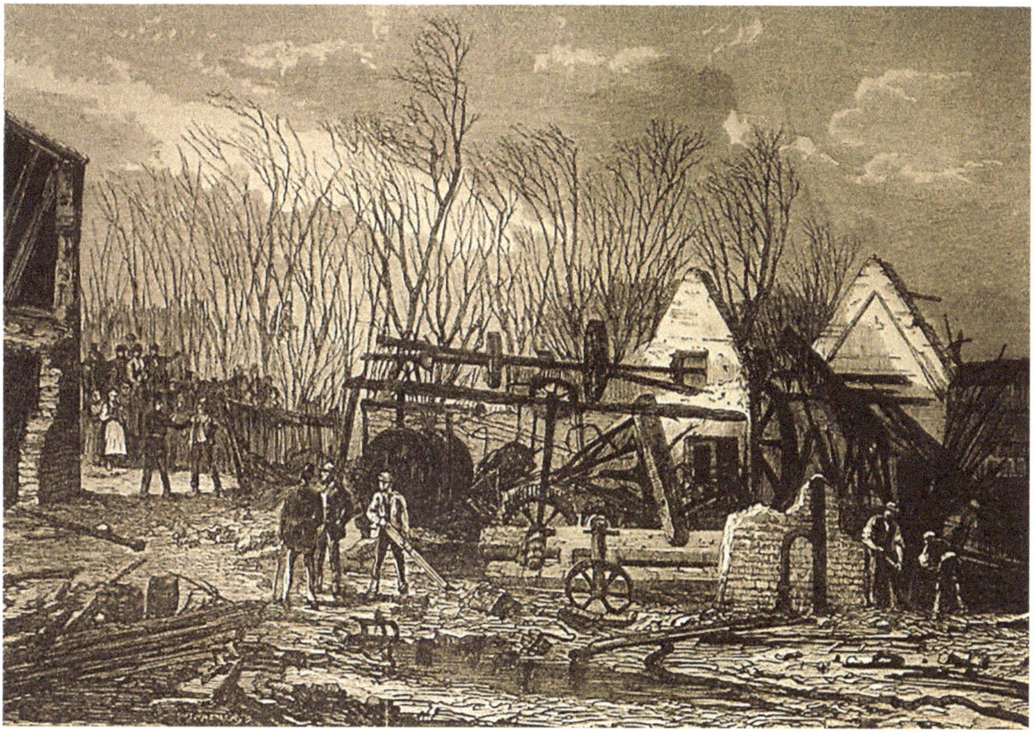

Aftermath of accidental explosion.

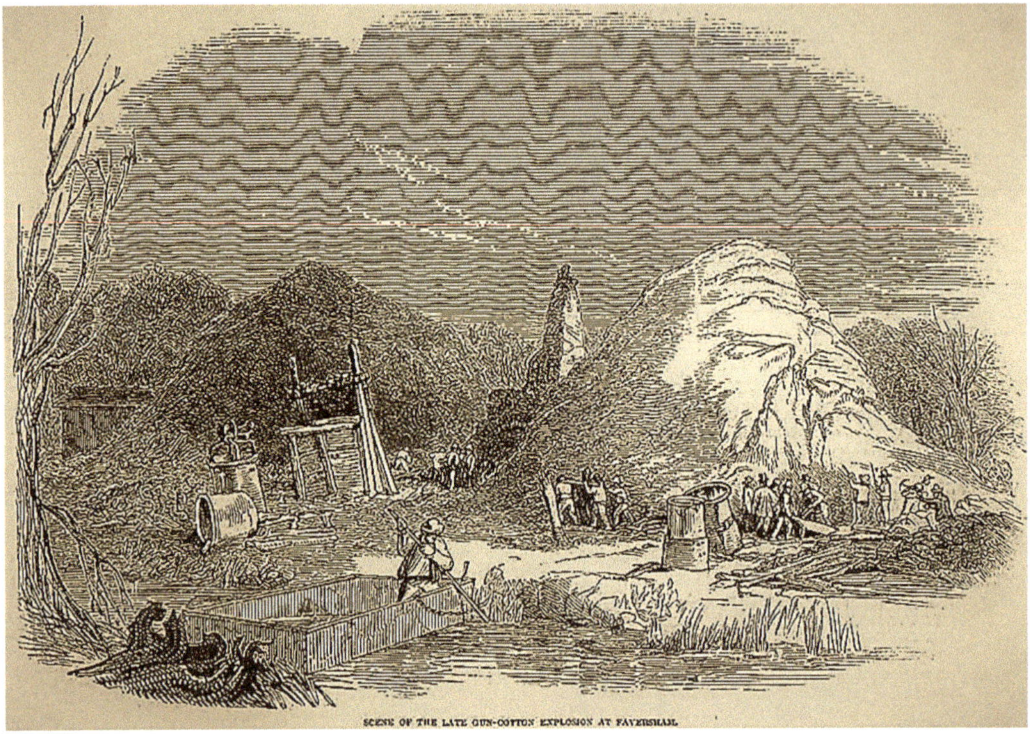

Devastated factory facilities.

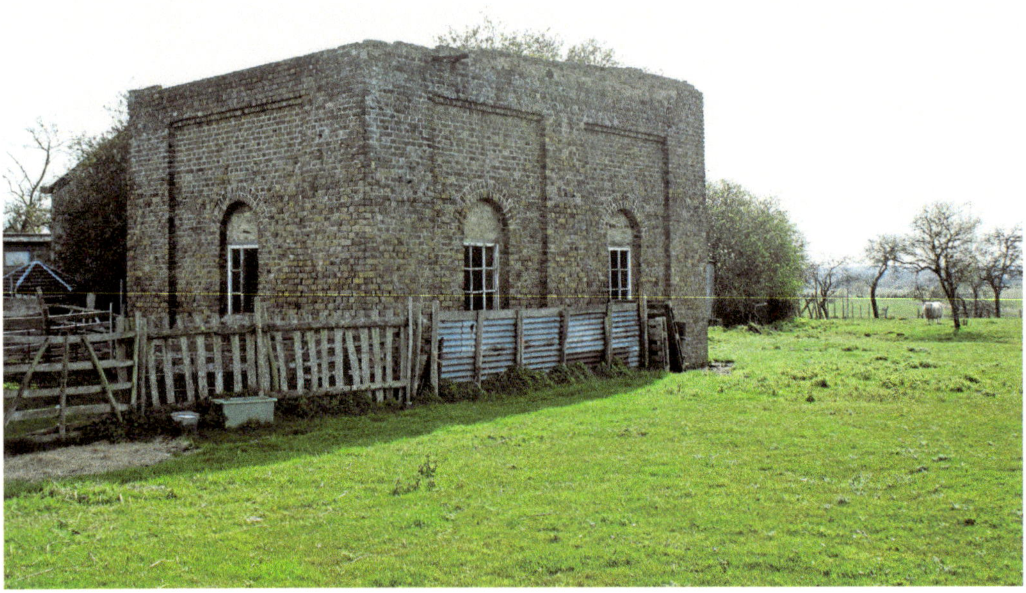

Sole surviving building at Uplees Works.

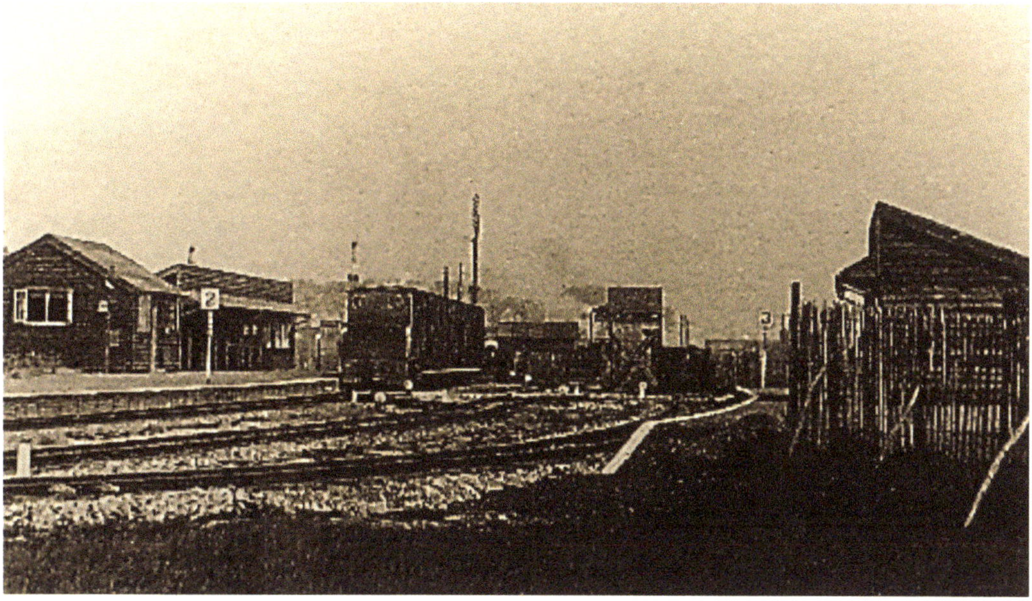

Railway track for transporting factory workers.

This was appropriately called the Explosives Loading Co. Overall the works by now covered a large area comprising over 500 acres (nearly a square mile). For safeties sake wide open spaces are a necessary requirement. This did not, however, prevent a huge accident later during the First World War.

At the outbreak of this event in 1914 the Admiralty requisitioned both sites. It increased output and recruited many new workers. To covey them to their occupations a light railway was constructed between Davington and Uplees. Existing road communication was poor.

In 1916, the massive explosion mentioned above occurred. Some 200 tons of TNT ignited killing 115 male workers. When it happened it was a Sunday, so no female workers were involved. The blast wave reverberated around the Thames Estuary with windows broken as far away as Southend in Essex. Bodies of the men that could be recovered were buried in a mass grave in Faversham Cemetery.

Explosive production at all these sites ceased in 1934 when ICI, who had become owners, realised that any future European war involving aerial combat would make Kent vulnerable.

Nonetheless, Faversham's long and estimable link to the explosive industry is kept alive by a small specialist firm called Cardox. It was set up as the Mining Explosives Company in 1924 on land at the east of the creek. It is known as Abbey Works due to its proximity to the old demolished abbey. A series of modest wooden huts belies the existence here of a most innovative and world-renowned firm.

Their product is a cleverly designed apparatus that is used extensively in the mining and engineering fields for unusual applications. Reusable metal tubes are filled with carbon dioxide, which is electronically detonated using a small explosive charge. The subsequent strength of blast is determined by the gauge of blank at the firing end of the cylinder. The major advantage of this device is that, unlike most explosives, subsequent shockwaves are confined to a precise area. Therefore, it can be used in difficult situations such as built-up populated sites.

Currently, there are five people employed in the manufacture of this highly specialised product at Abbey Works.

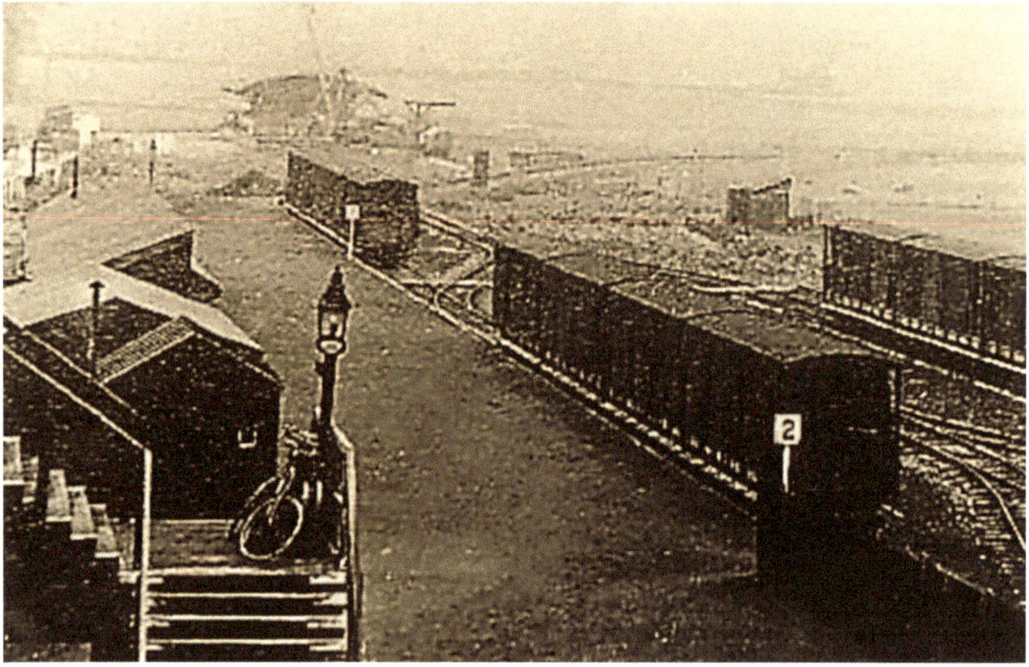

Rudimentary passenger carriages.

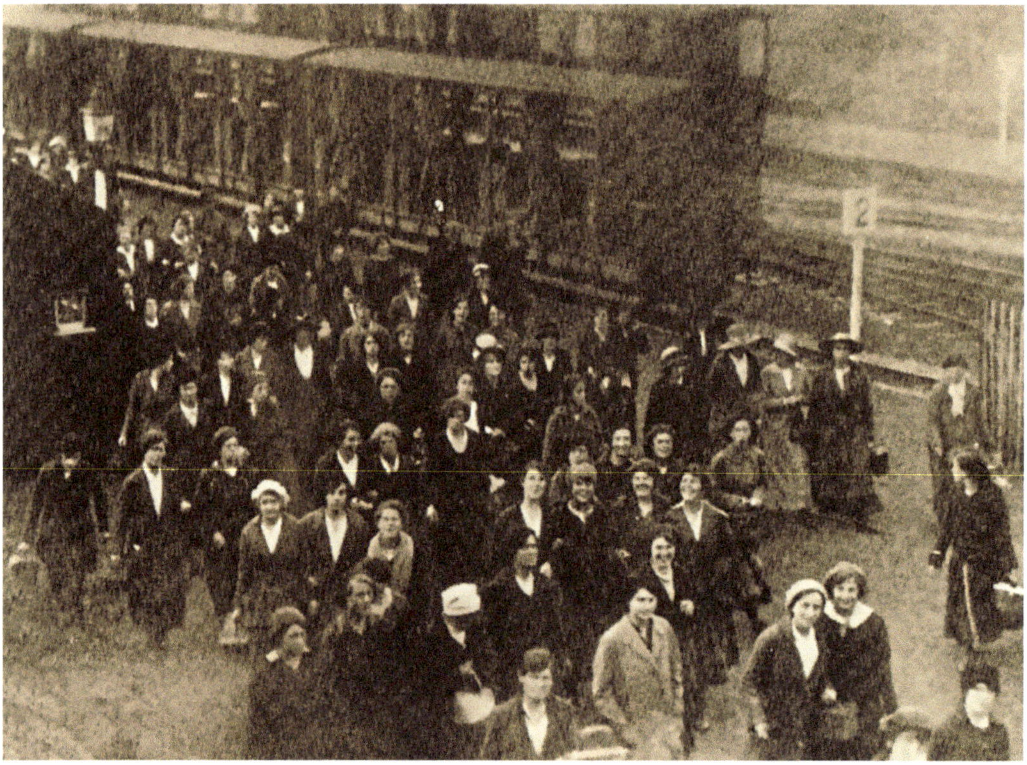

Army of women swarming to factory jobs.

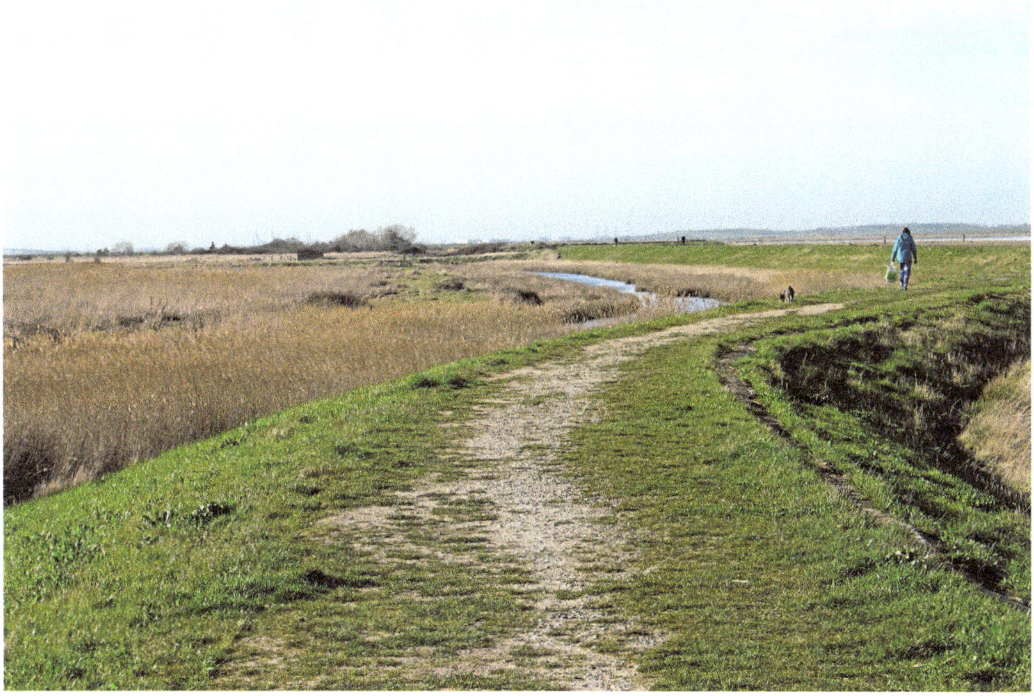

Nature reasserts itself at Uplees.

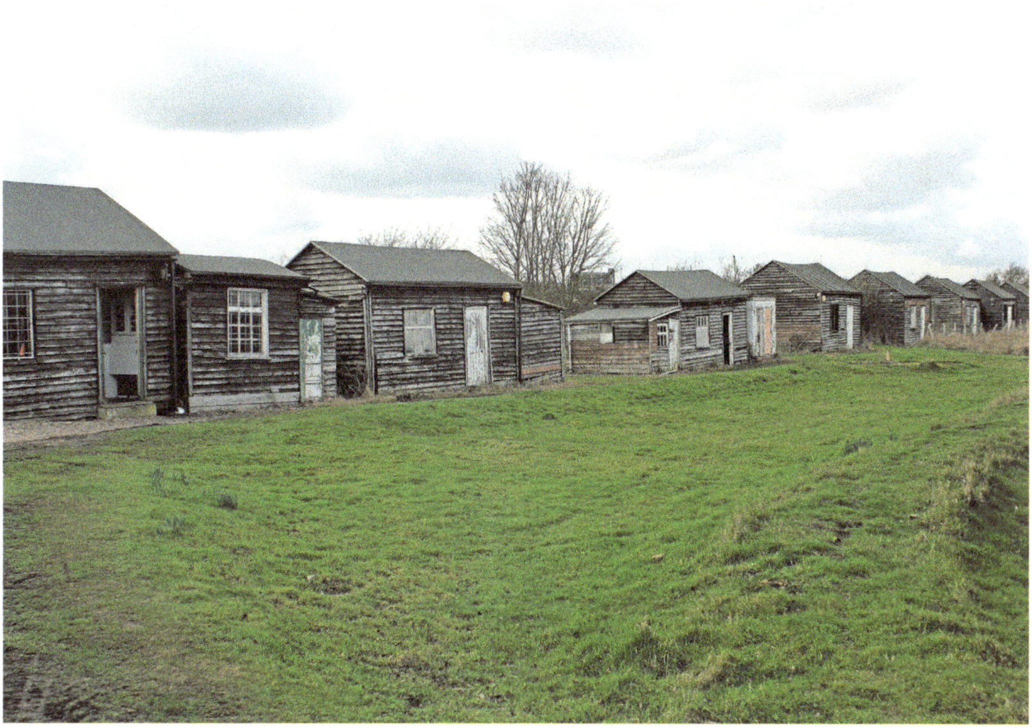

Huts at Cardox's Abbey Works.

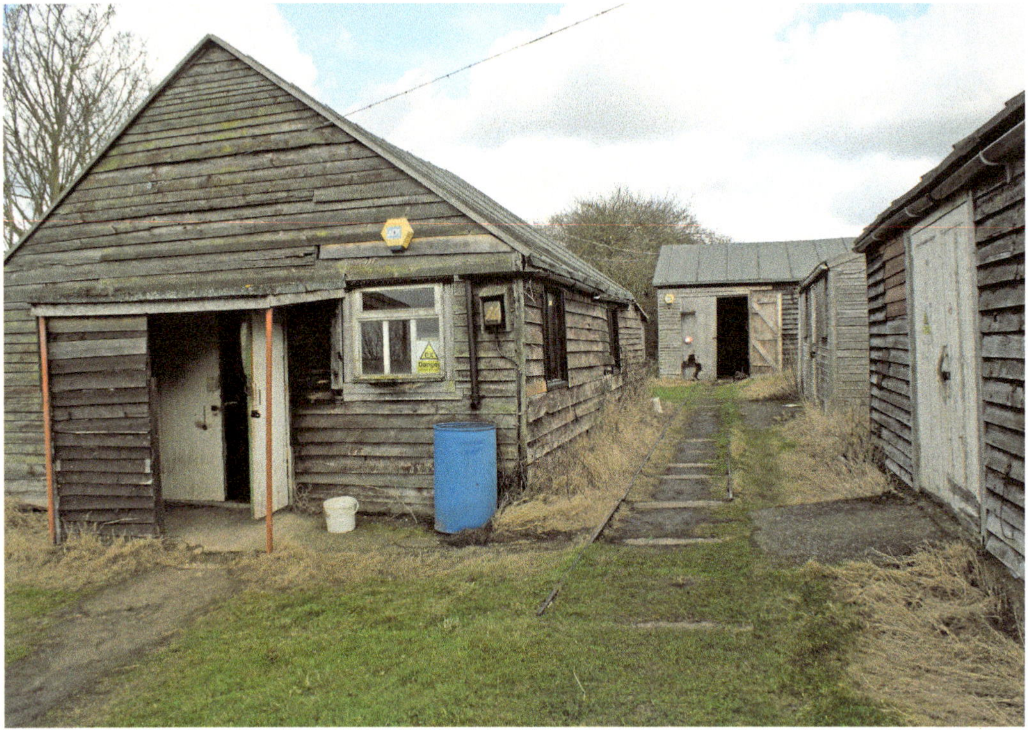

Redundant rail track.

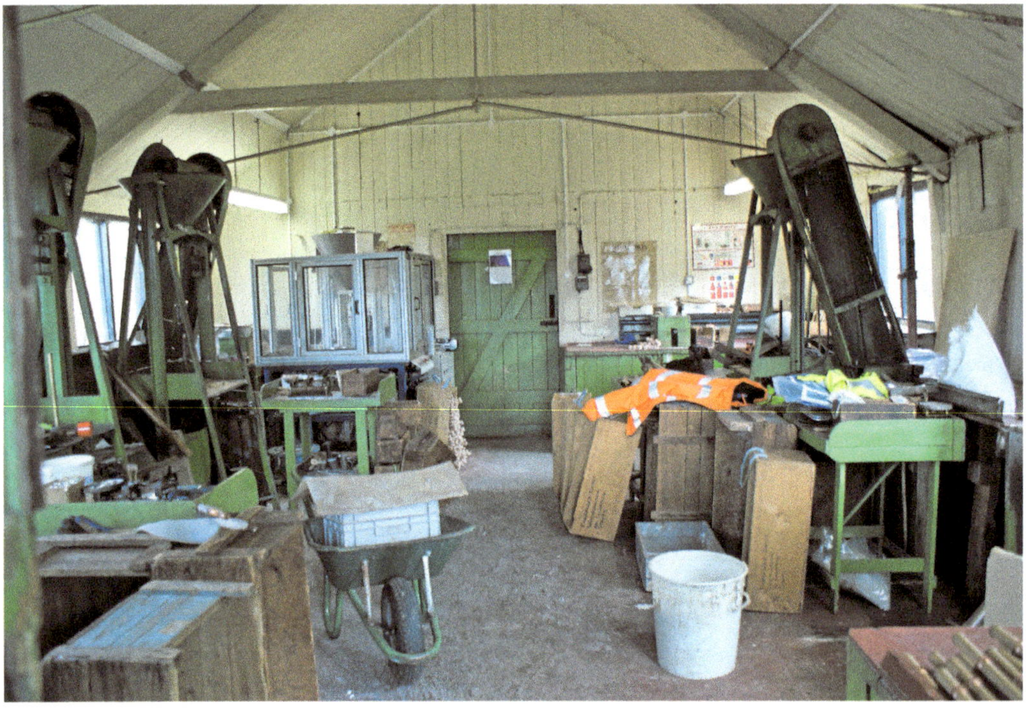

Factory machinery.

BREWING

Kent is famous for its hops and Faversham, with its fertile soils and kind climate, is an ideal location for their cultivation. Considered a pernicious weed in medieval times, vast acreages reached an apogee in the Victorian era. Distinctive hop gardens with high trellises once surrounded this town. Frequently dotted among them were conical-shaped buildings called oast houses. They were used for drying the recently picked pungent green flower heads.

Presently large quantities of hops are imported from Eastern Europe, but some dedicated local growers have survived and flourish. Most oast houses, however, are now invariably converted into luxury homes.

Brewing in Faversham has its origins in the twelfth century. The enormous abbey founded by King Stephen in 1147 had its own brewhouse, which provided ale for the monks. It was built over a well from which pure chalk-filtered water could be drawn.

Later in the fourteenth century it was recorded that almost 100 alewives were making and selling beer from either their homes or inns.

By 1525 the brother of the last abbot of Faversham was involved in exporting and importing beer. His name was William Castlock and his son John followed him in this occupation. The latter acquired No. 18 Court Street in 1570. This site, now owned by Shepherd Neame, is where brewing has taken place continuously thereafter. John Castlock's grandson was barred from brewing by Faversham's strict Parliamentarian Corporation in 1648. Perhaps this is why ownership then passed to Thomas Hilton.

Then in 1678 Richard Marsh took over. He was a prominent burgher who when mayor held James II captive at his brewery while on his flight of escape to the Continent. Originally he leased the premises, but in 1698 bought them outright – thus marking the start of Britain's oldest brewery.

In 1732, Samuel Shepherd married into the Marsh family. He headed the business, which entered a strong period of growth. Vertical economic integration towards the market was implemented by enlarging the firm's portfolio of pubs. Julius (Samuel's son) followed in his father's footsteps and is credited with introducing mechanisation. He installed a revolutionary steam engine in the late eighteenth century. It came from the Birmingham works of legendary engineers James Watt and Matthew Boulton.

During the 1800s, a new partner, John Mares, joined. His son in-law Percy Neame, a hop farmer, came on board in 1864 and so Shepherd Neame & Co. was formed. Renewed management vigour ensued with a better brewhouse and stores erected. Additionally, pub ownership expanded to nearly 100.

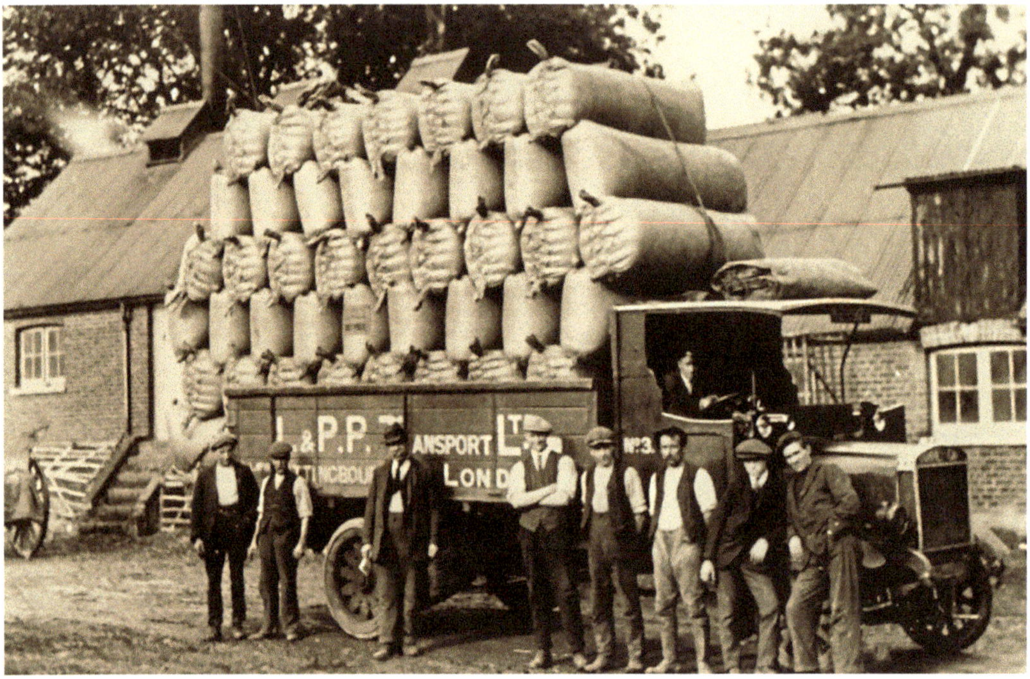

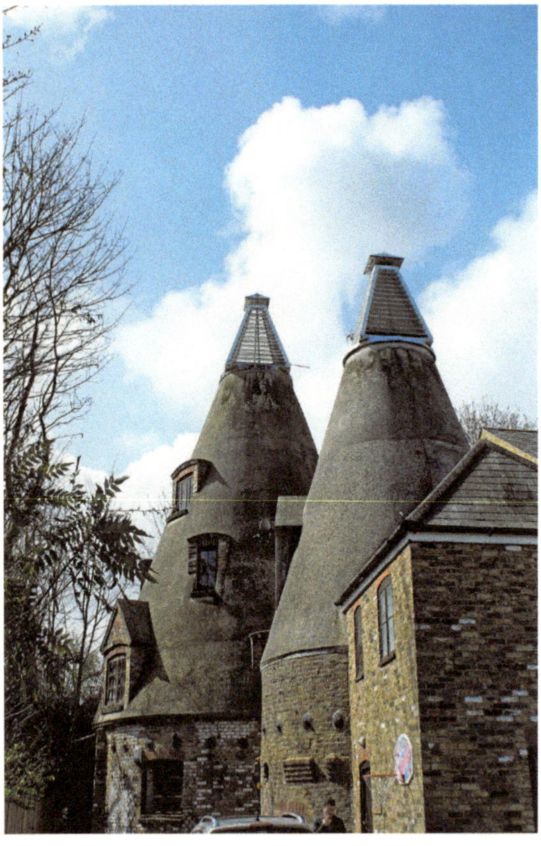

Above: Hops leaving grower.

Left: Converted oast houses.

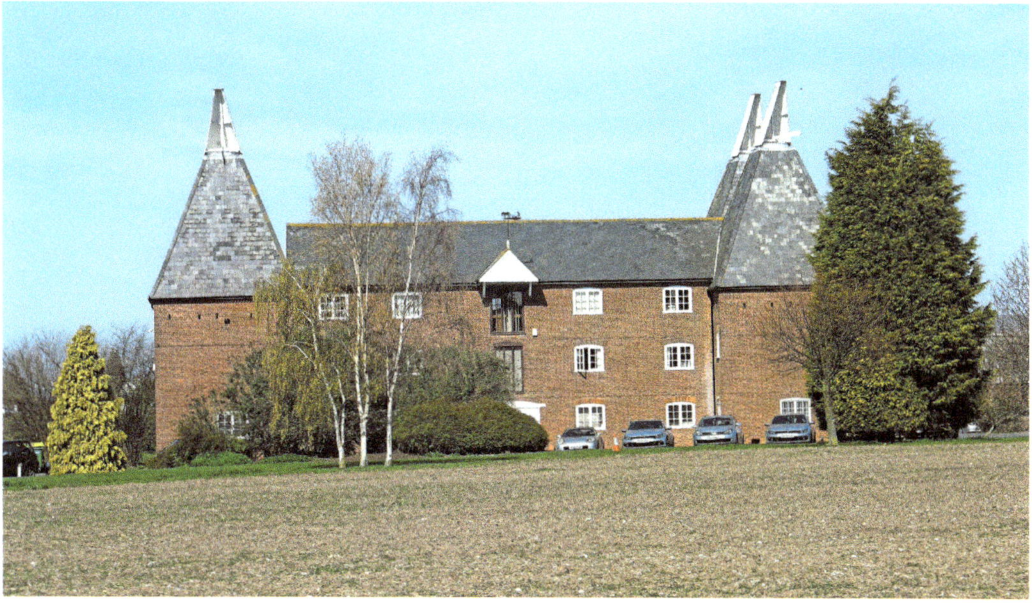

Oast complex, Brogdale.

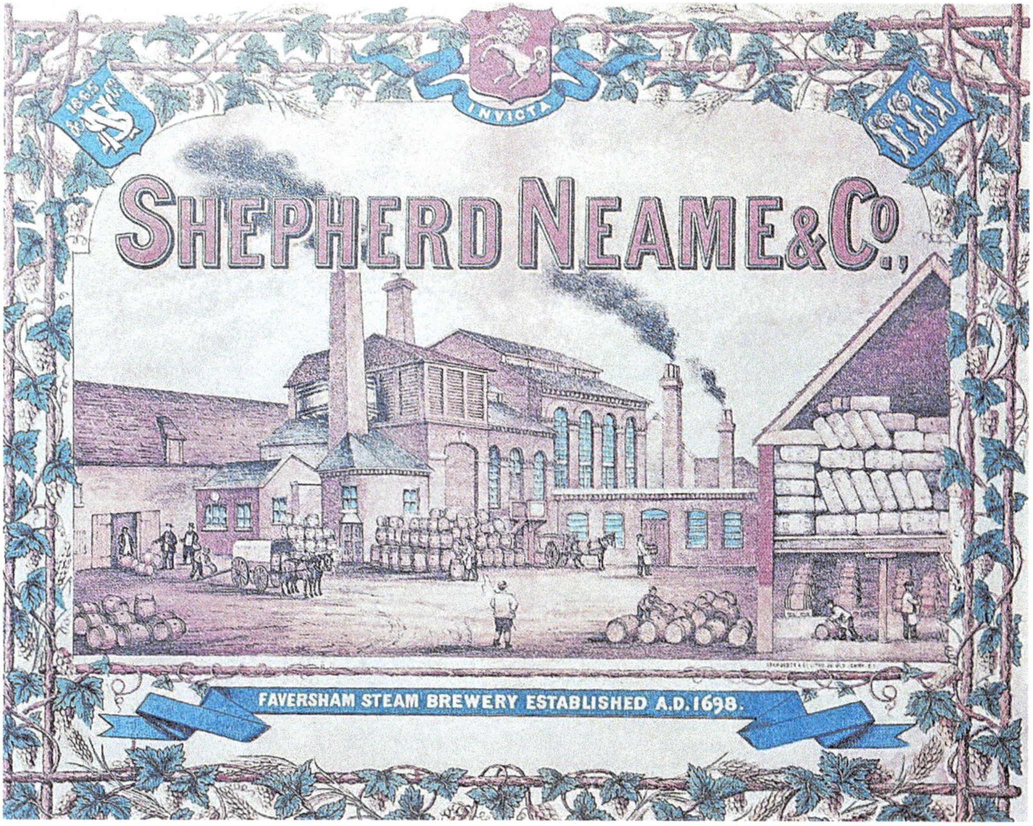

Label illustrating 'Sheps' Steam Brewery.

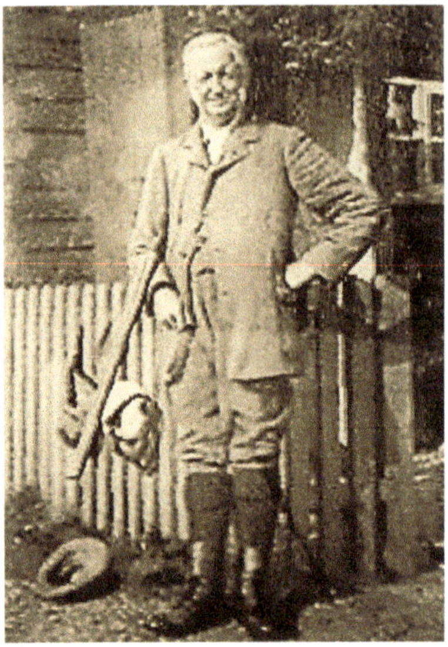

Percy Neame.

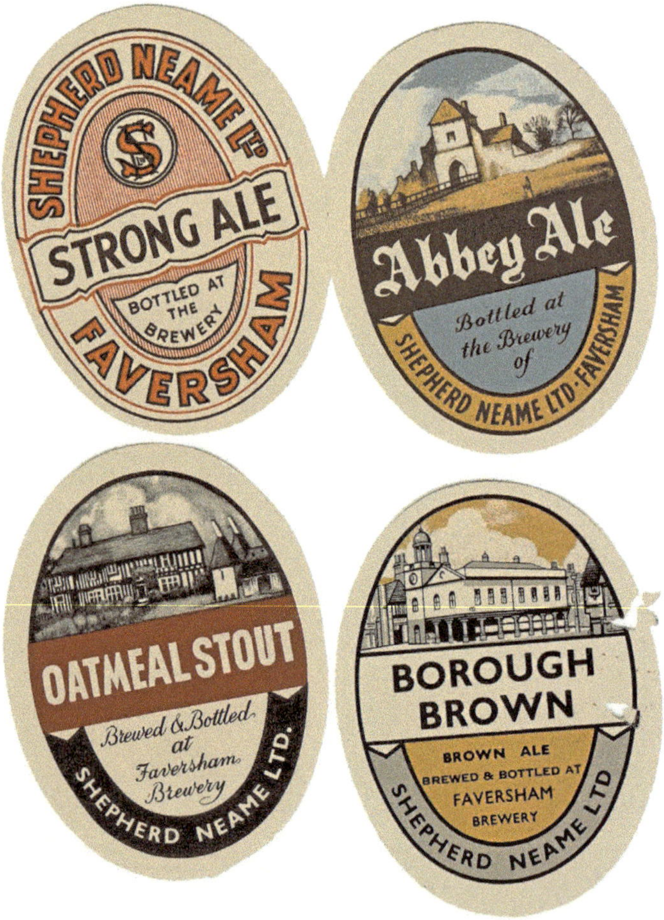

Shepherd Neame brand advertising beer mats.

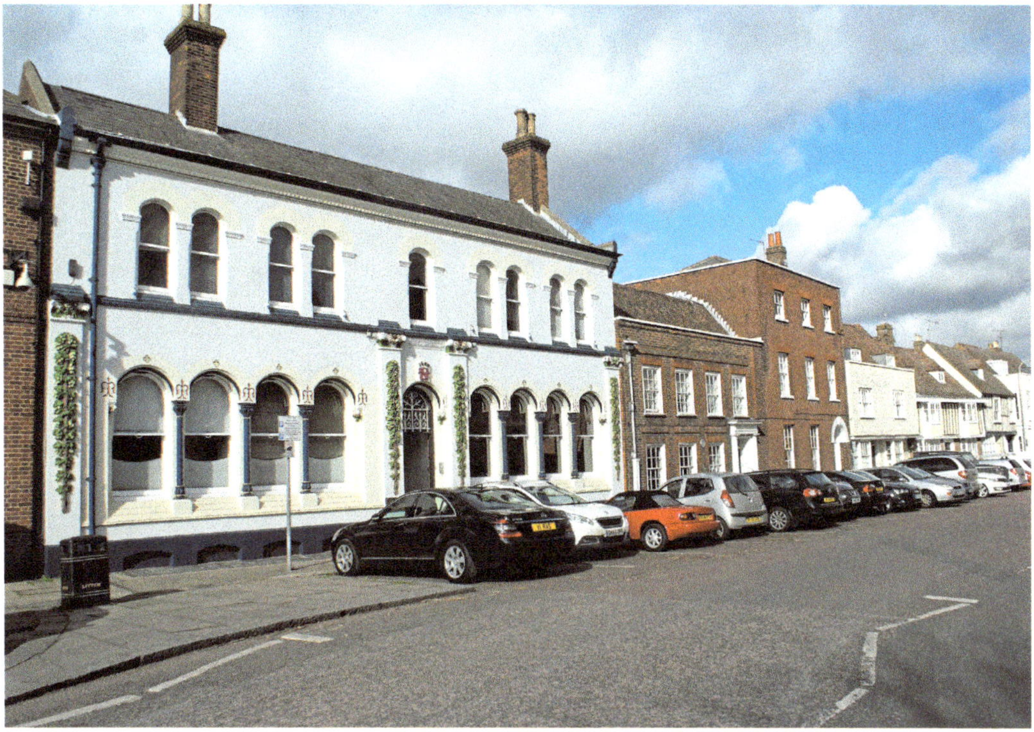

Administration headquarters of Shepherd Neame, Court Street.

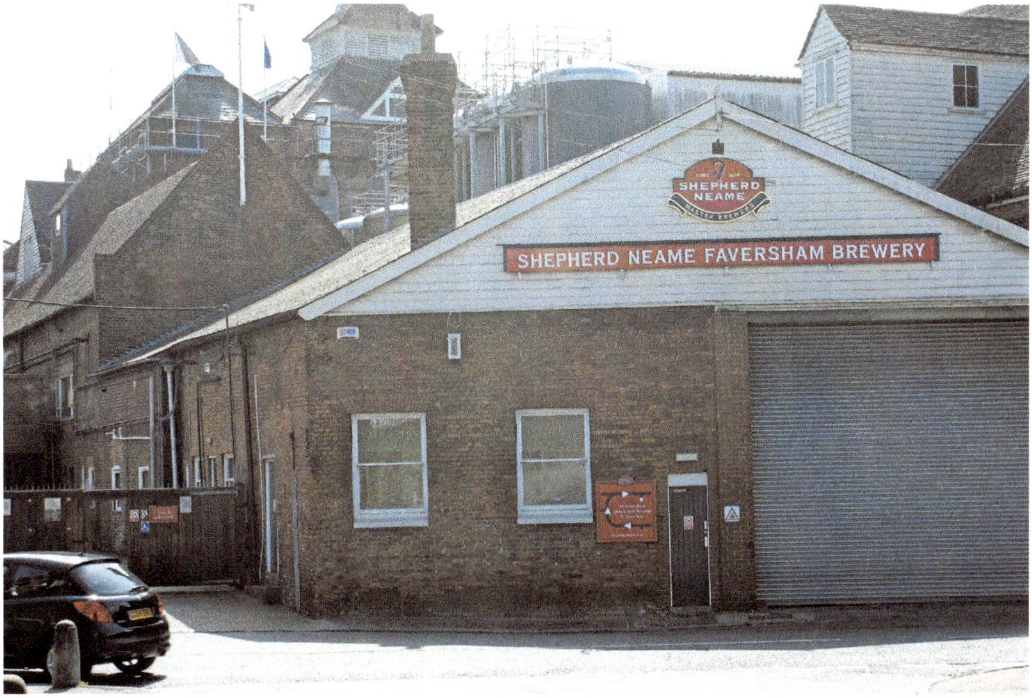

Production side of business.

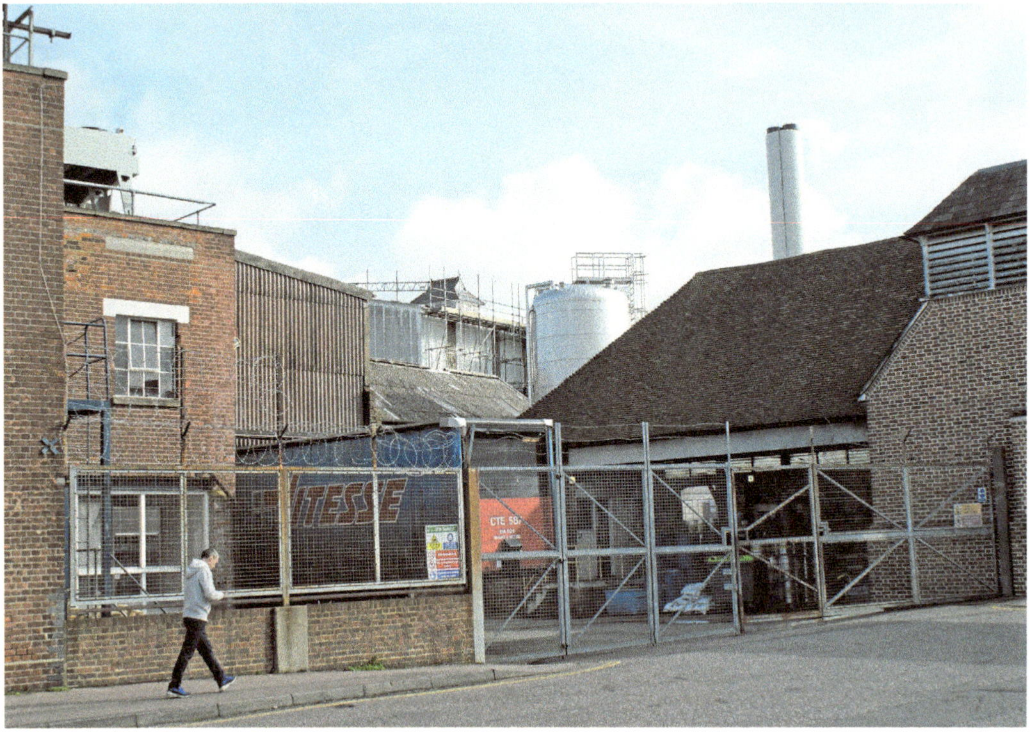

Brewing infrastructure.

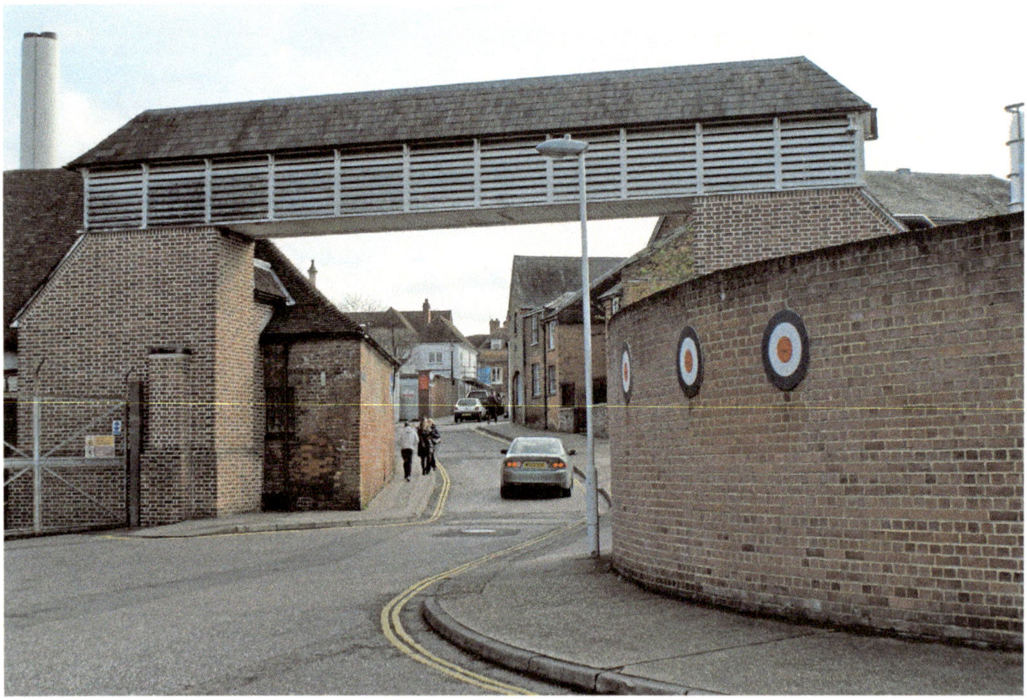

RAF insignia at the loading bay referencing Spitfire beer brand.

As direction passed from generation to generation of the Neame family, success built on success. This company is today a highly profitable go-ahead concern. It has a number of well-promoted brands that, despite the overall national decline in beer consumption, have kept turnover rising; notably the cheekily advertised Spitfire, which has gained many loyal devotees. In summation, 'Sheps', as it is affectionately known, has become synonymous with Faversham. It is a significant and well-regarded employer.

The other major brewery based opposite was founded by Edward Rigden in the early eighteenth century. It merged with the very appropriately named George Beer of Canterbury in 1922. Fremlins of Maidstone took over this organisation and was in turn absorbed into Whitbread. Perceiving Costa Coffee and Premier Inns to be more profitable than brewing, Whitbread withdrew from this industry altogether and, as a consequence of this strategic decision, its factory at Faversham closed in 1990.

Tesco supermarket has adopted the main buildings without detracting from their elegant red-brick elevations. Such policies have been a hallmark of the careful concern residents have shown to the conservation of their attractive environs.

Microbrewing is a relatively new phenomenon. Faversham has its own representative of this emerging trend at Brogdale. Here the Mad Cat Brewery is ably run by Peter and Mike Meany. Production has currently reached 2,000 casks (9 gallons capacity) per annum. Distribution to customers is along a corridor between Folkestone and Woolwich. Supporting local agriculture, Goldings hops are supplied by John and Anna Clinch of Syndale Farm.

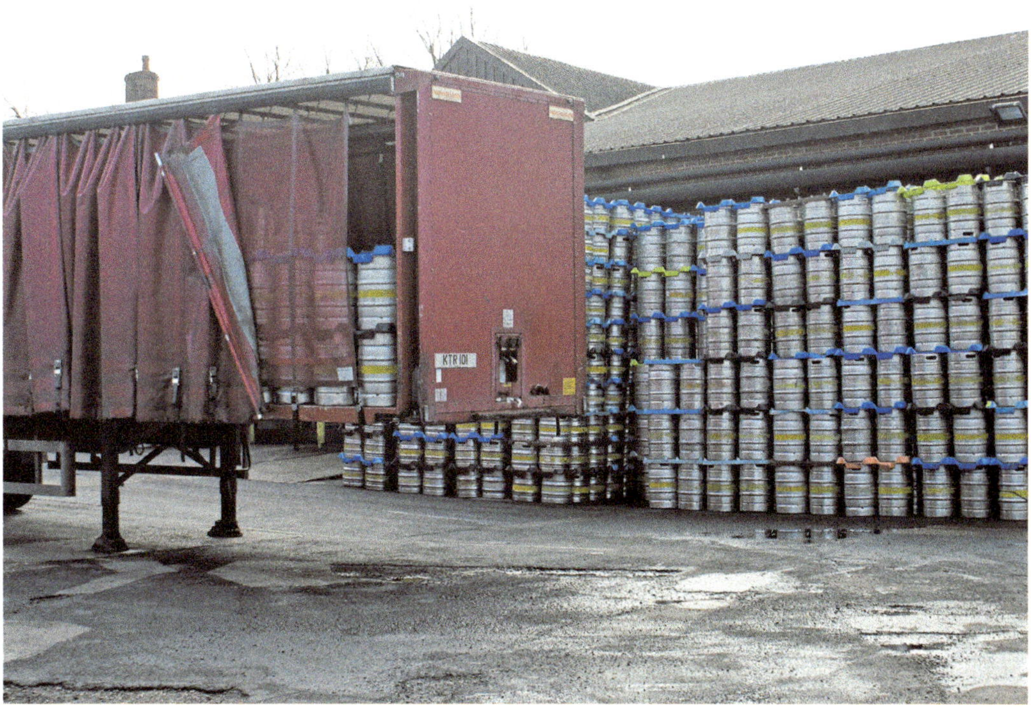

Full kegs stacked before distribution.

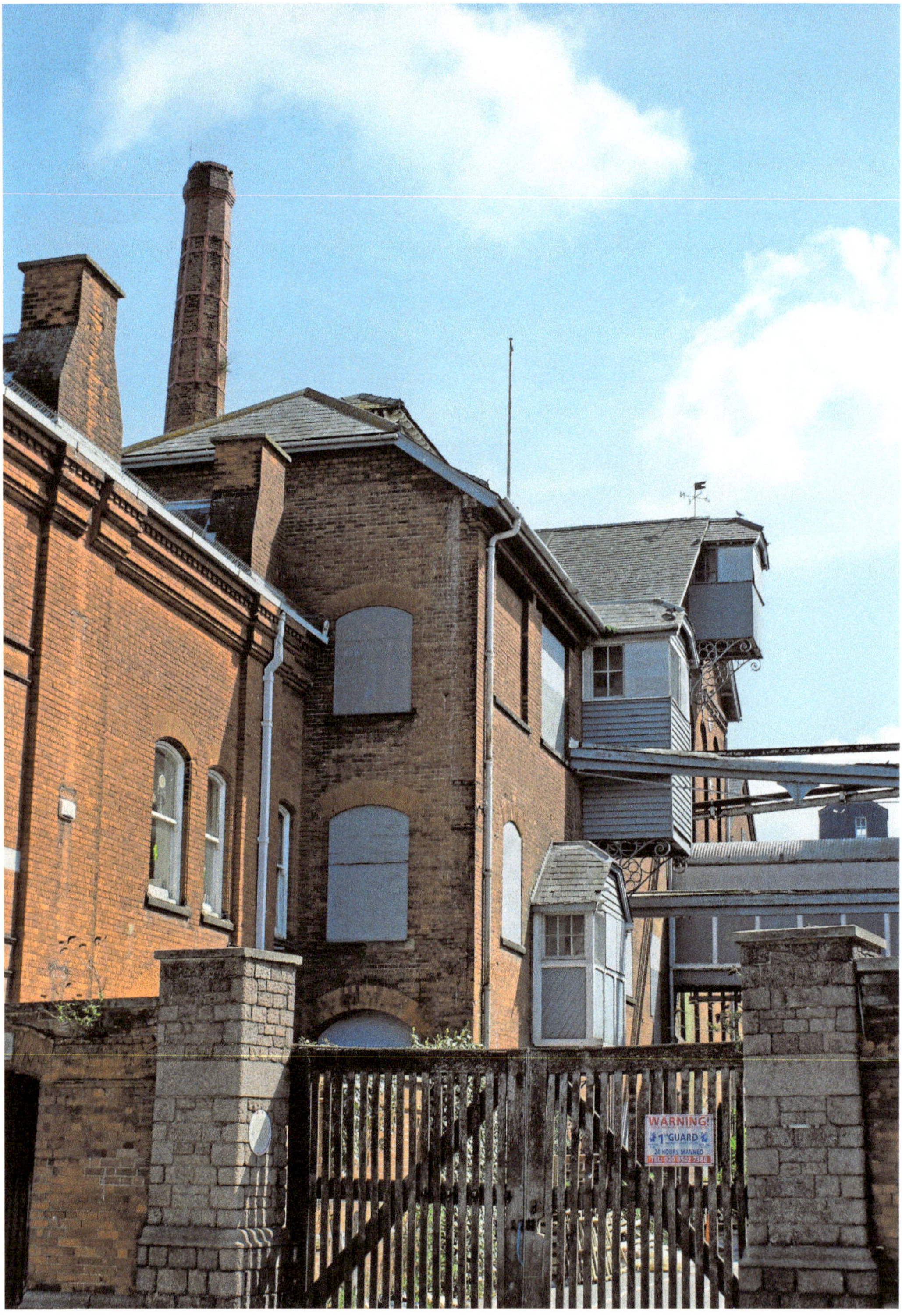

Whitbread's redundant factory buildings.

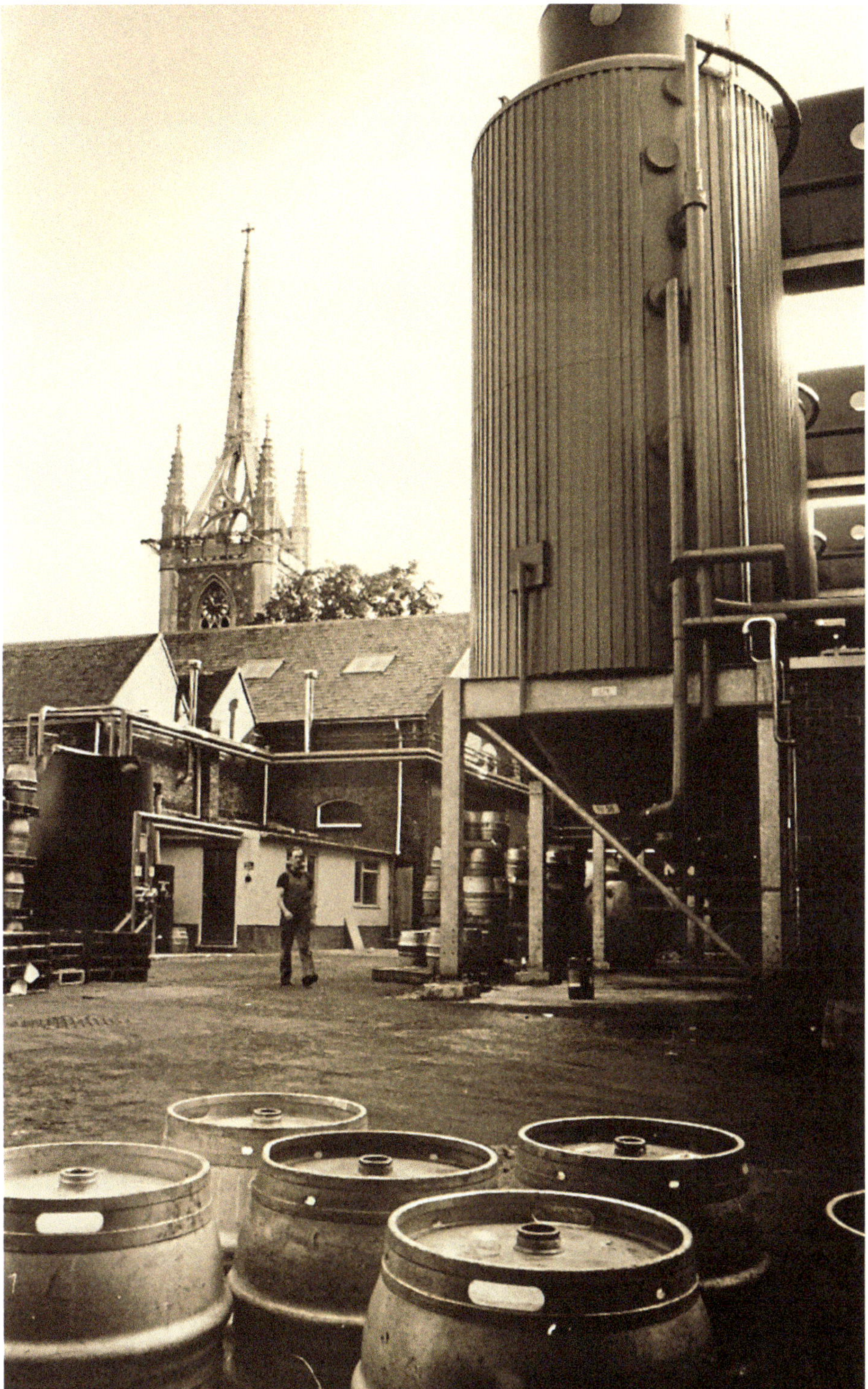

Whitbread's Brewery during operation.

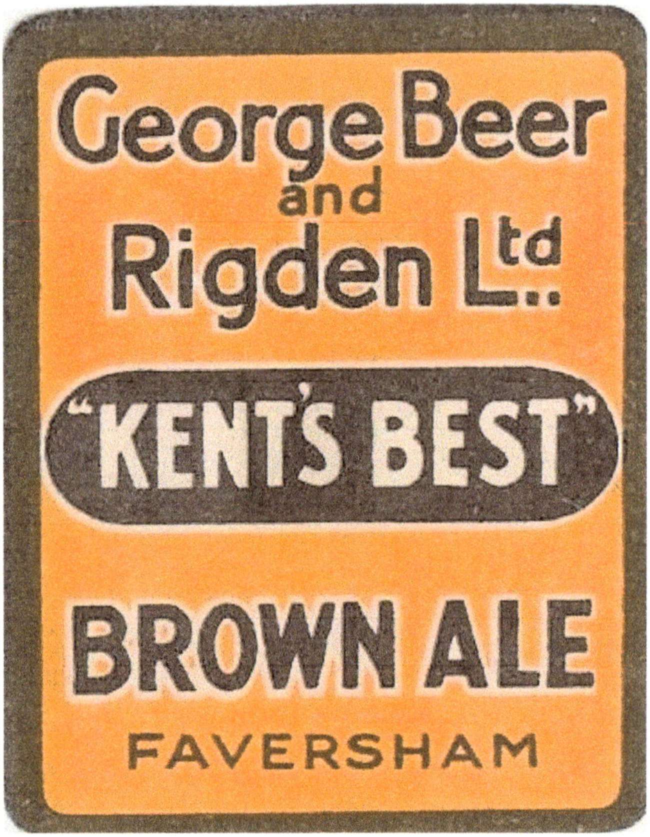

Left: Beer mat of Whitbread's predecessors.

Below: Rigden's pub in Ospringe Road.

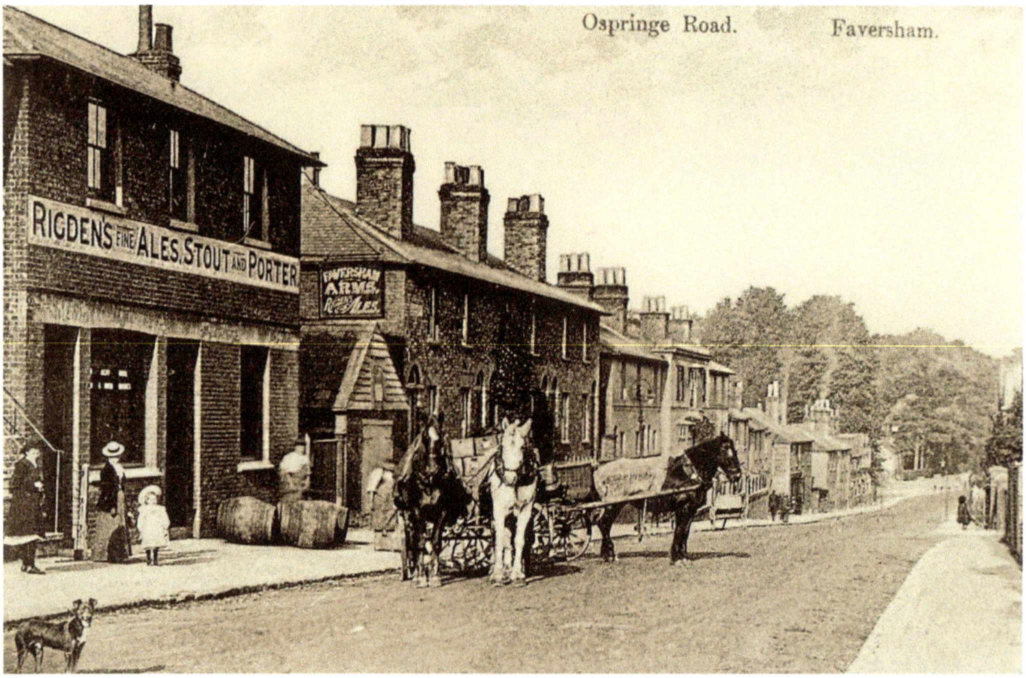

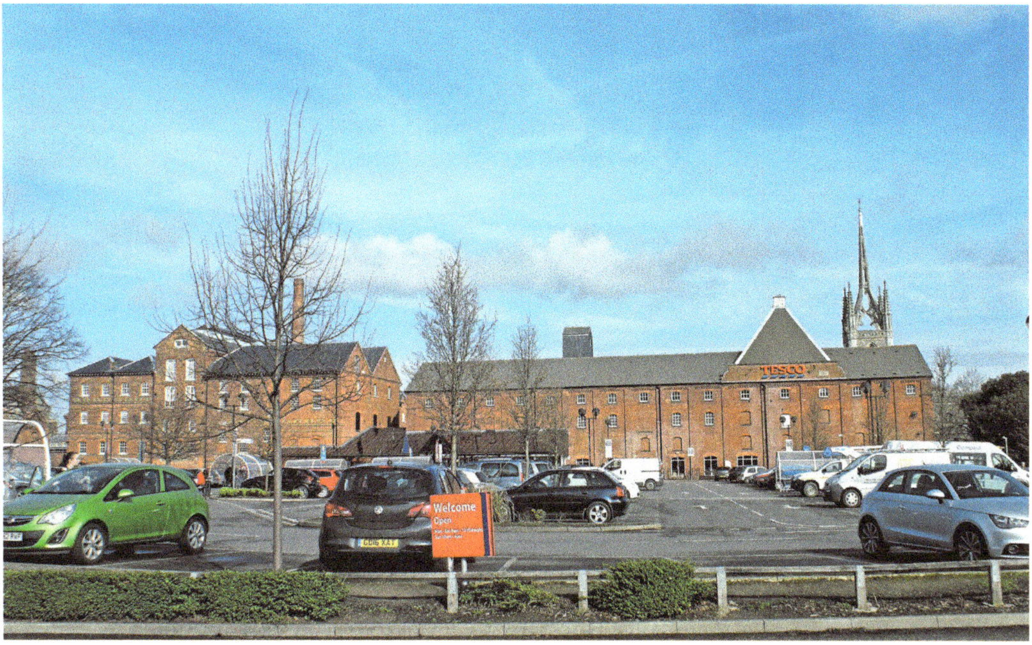

Above: Tesco's supermarket converted from Whitbread Brewery.

Right: Microbrewing at Brogdale.

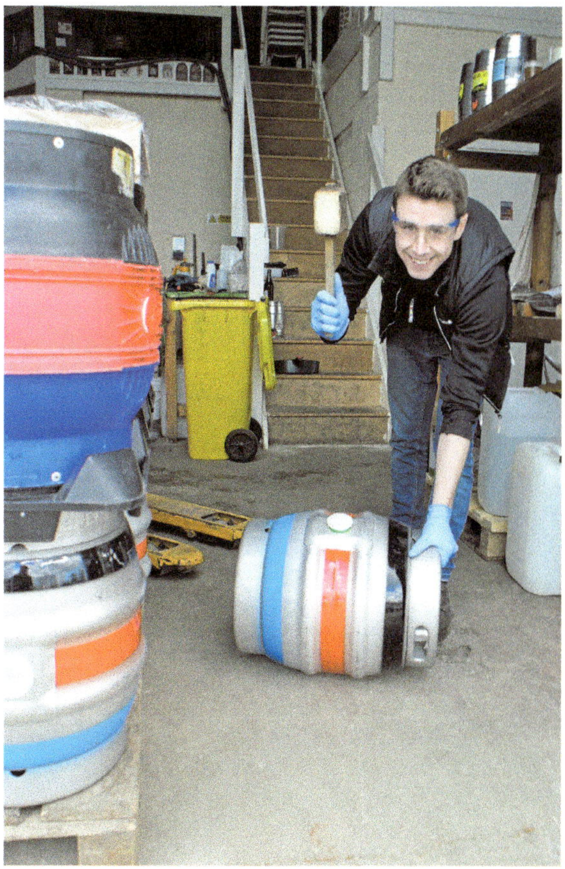

BRICK MAKING

Brick making has made an enormous contribution to Faversham's economic history and to a lesser degree is still part of the towns overall industrial activity.

Bricks are one of the earliest known building materials, dating back to 7000 BC. The Romans who had a settlement at Faversham, called Durolevum (fortress by a stream), were using them here from around AD 40. For a long period after the Romans departed there was no brick making in this country as Saxons preferred to use timber for constructing buildings. The monasteries did, however, reintroduce the craft and by Elizabethan times wealthier yeomen were commonly having chimney stacks installed. Following the Great Fire of London wide scale general usage occurred.

At this time bricks were often made close to the buildings they were to become. The laborious job of digging earth, mixing it and shaping it, then drying and firing was executed by the bricklayers themselves.

By the eighteenth, and particularly the nineteenth century, the whole process was on a much bigger scale – albeit still very hard labour-intensive work. Geologically, Faversham could not have been better placed for this vitally important industry. It was surrounded by loam or brick earth, laying above a strata of chalk. These two ingredients plus ash were the basic ingredients of yellow stock bricks. The proportions were as follows: 64 per cent brick earth, 25 per cent ash and 11 per cent chalk. This combination produced an extremely durable product, which tended to become even harder over time. The process of manufacture started with earth and chalk being pumped with water into 'washbacks' to dry and become pug. Then ash was added and, after this combination, the malleable clay was hand formed into bricks and later dried before firing. Gangs of six formed operational teams made up of three men, one youth and two boys. They were paid piecework and employers formed a cartel over rates of pay.

Due to potential frost and other inclement weather most output was confined to summer months and it is not difficult to comprehend what a tough, insecure livelihood this must have been, particularly for women and children engaged in sifting London rubbish for ash at quaysides.

When in 1824 the government passed legislation inaugurating the railway age, a mania to develop them started immediately. Stockton–Darlington and Canterbury–Whitstable were the earliest because their tracks were easily laid, traversing open countryside. However, to realistically operate in built-up areas brick viaducts were required. And so when the first metropolitan line from London Bridge to Greenwich was planned it ran over 878 arches on

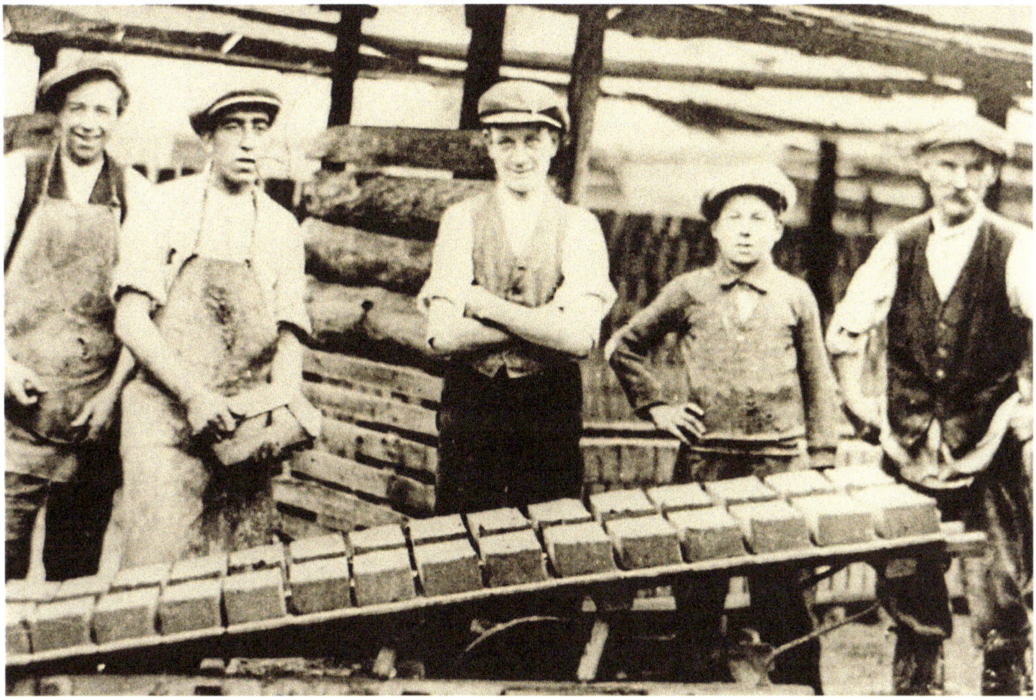

North Kent brick making team.

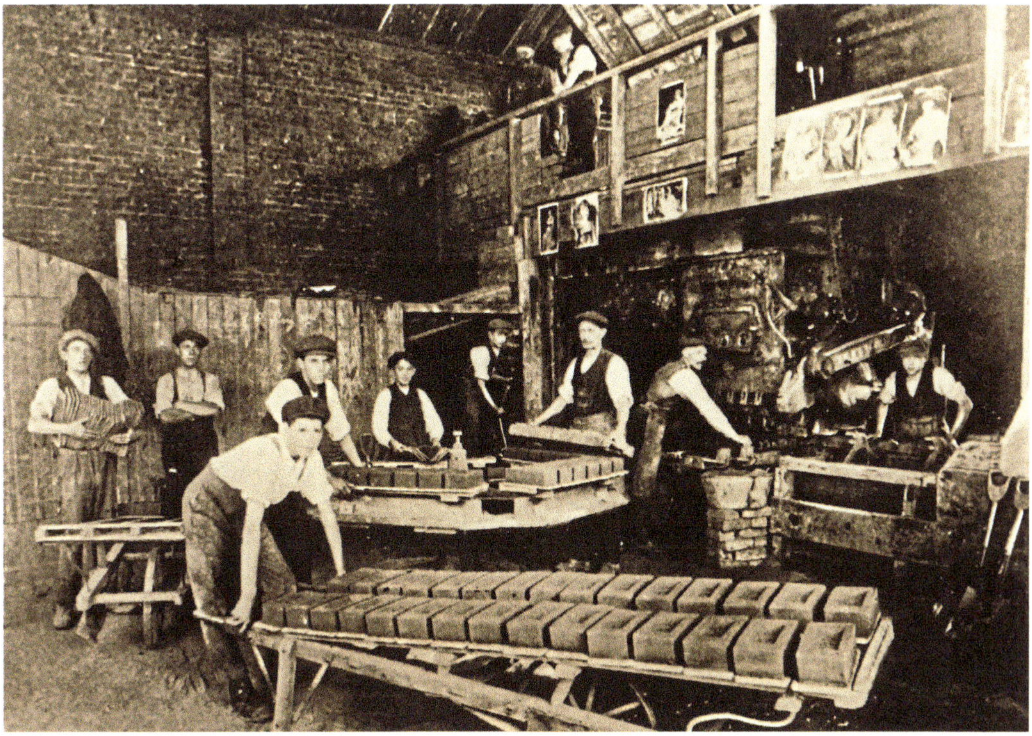

Loading bricks onto barrows.

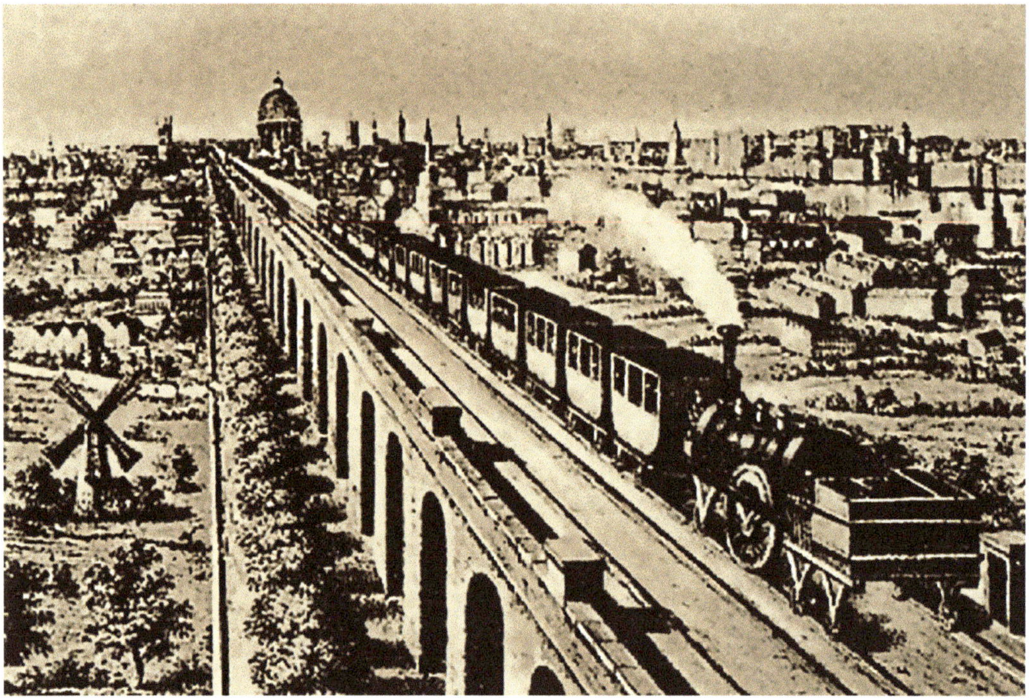

Brick viaduct from London Bridge to Greenwich.

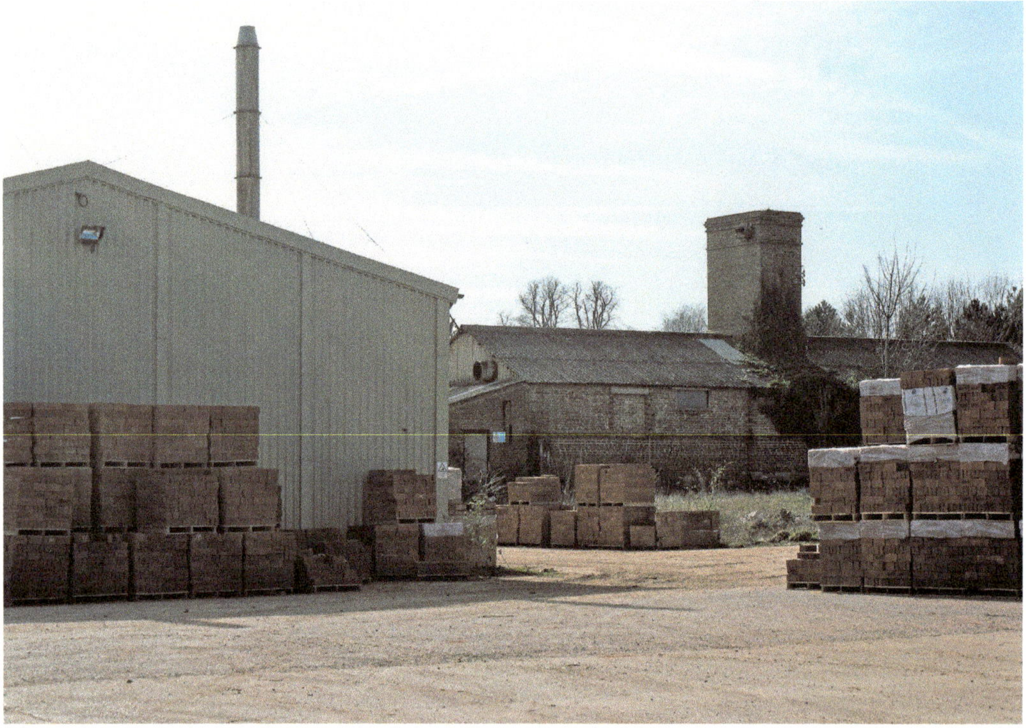

Faversham's sole remaining brick factory.

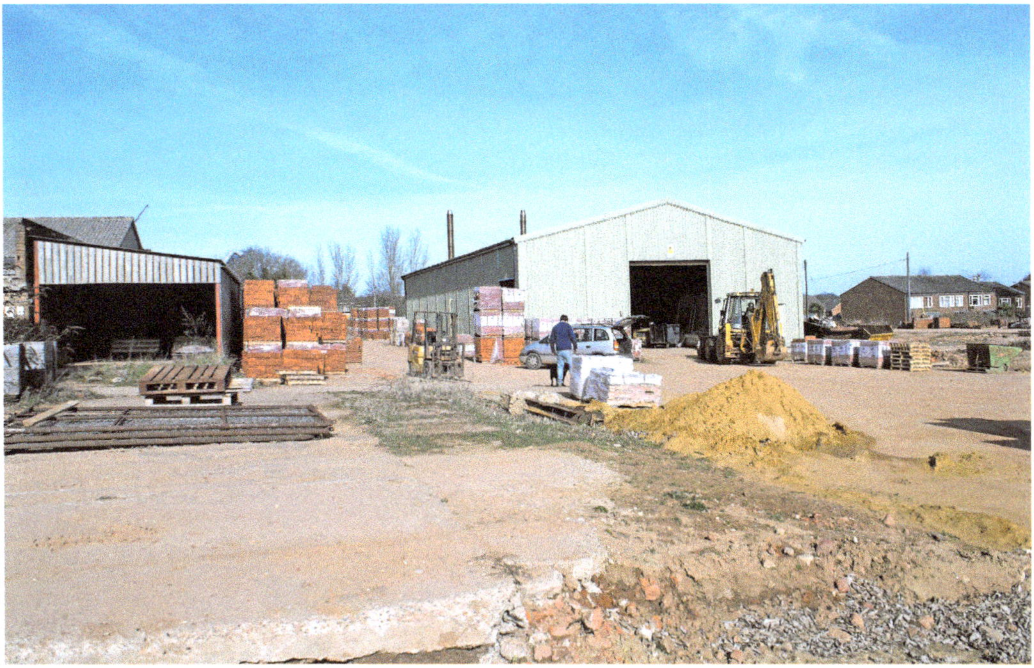

Cremer and Whiting's kiln building.

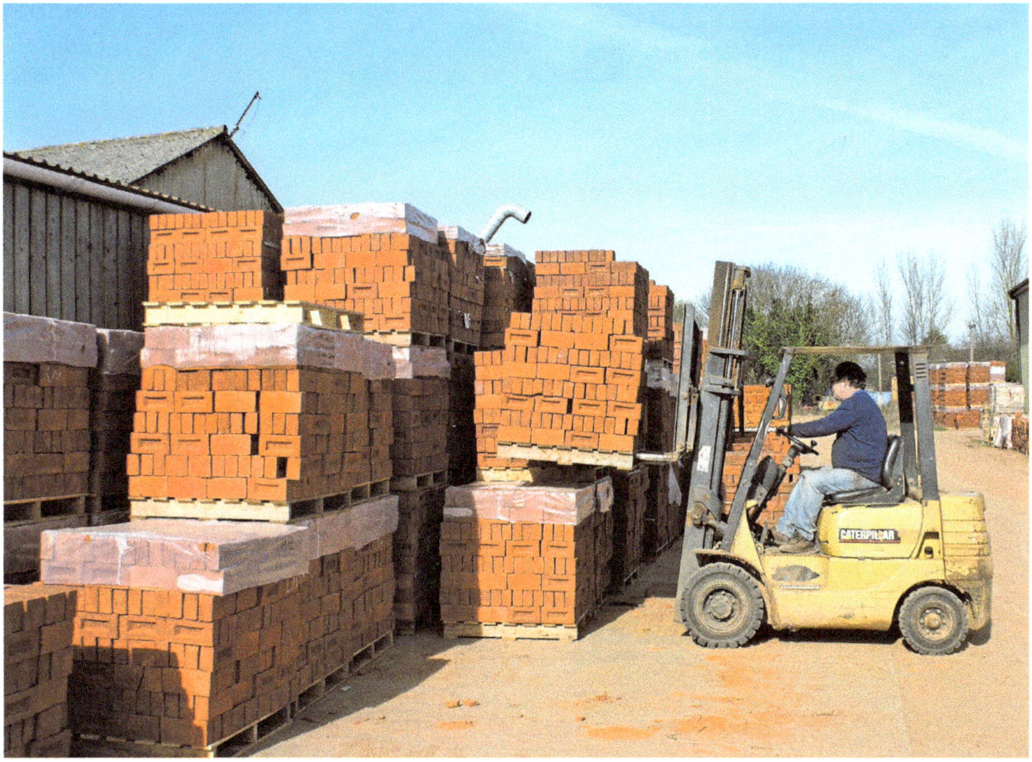

Distinctively red Kent bricks stacked for customer delivery.

its nearly 4-mile route. Staggeringly every one of the 100,000 bricks laid per day by 400 men came by sailing barge from Faversham. The quality of materials and workmanship has endured, as this author can testify to having commuted for decades over this 'highway' into the city by train.

In the late 1800s, local sources of brick earth had started to become exhausted. Also competition from a new type of brick called flettons, made cheaply in the Midlands, presaged decline.

Only Cremer and Whiting are extant today. They still operate on a site close to the railway line over towards Bysing Woods. Special products made here include bricks for restoration projects and odd shapes for decoration or coping courses. The old chimney of the coal-fired redundant kiln survives. It has been replaced by two gas-fired ones. In past times there was a siding from the main rail track delivering coal supplies and facilitating movement of finished output. Such was the scale of previous operations that there was also a light railway with steam locomotives taking bricks north for embarkation on barges – 40,000 per cargo.

Long-standing colleagues Barry Parkes and Richard Todd can be seen in the contemporary snapshots. Also pictured overleaf are ancient items of jewellery, which were over the years found in excavated brickfields and are now kept in the British Museum.

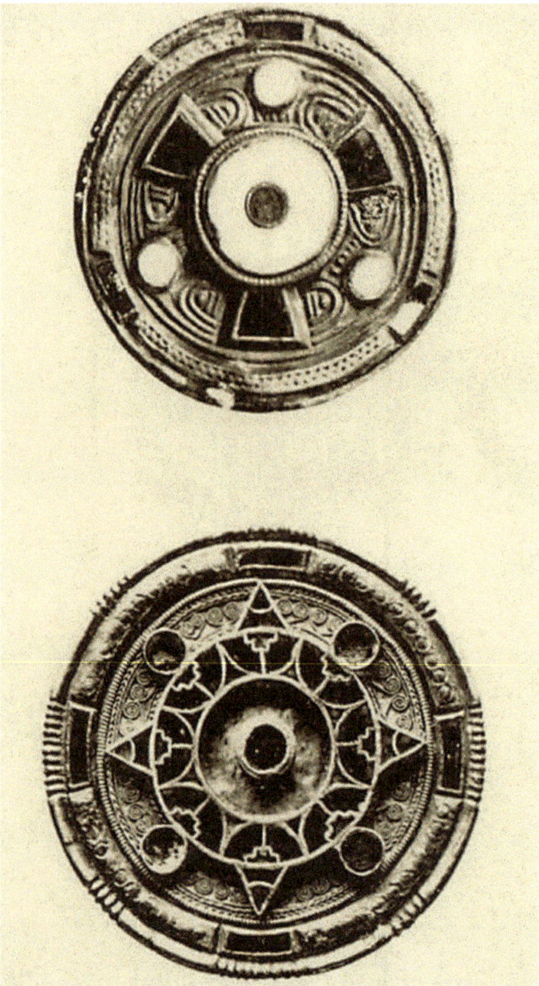

Ancient jewellery finds from brickfields.

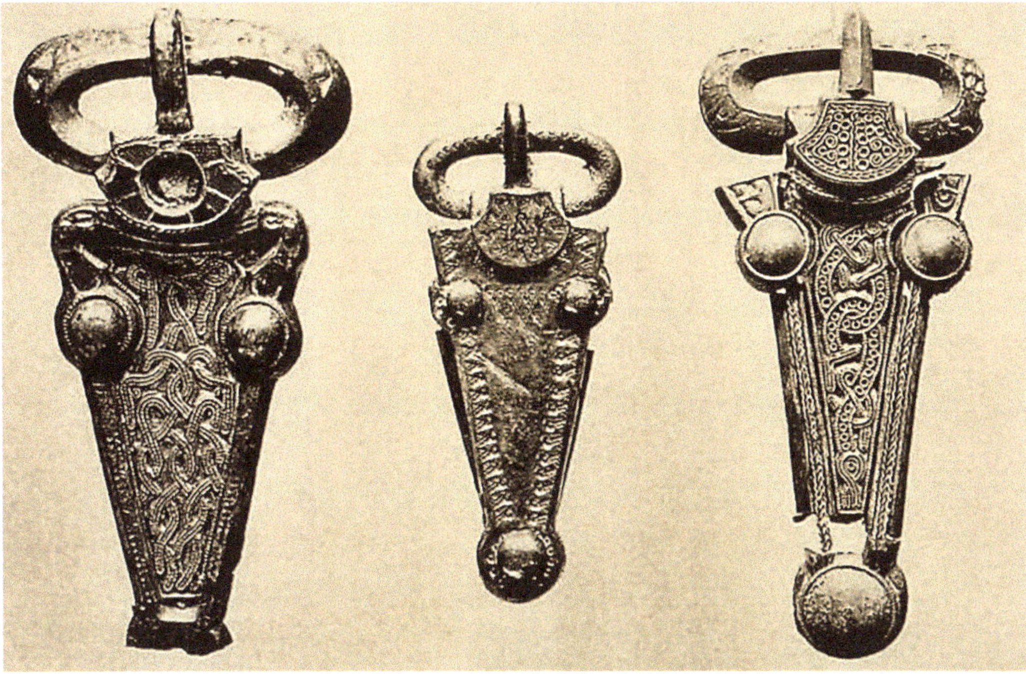

Above: Ornate buckles preserved for centuries in brick earth.

Right: Cremer and Whiting brick makers.

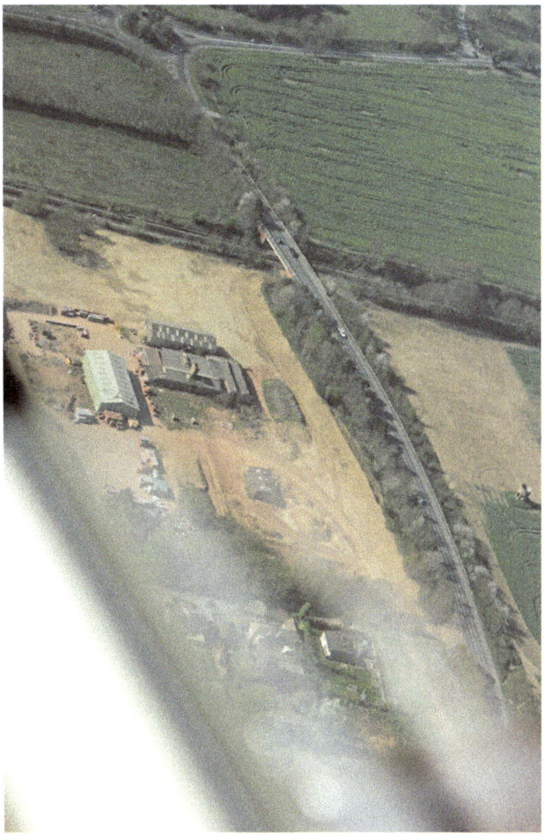

BOAT BUILDING AND REPAIRS

Faversham already had an important maritime role before it became a limb of the Cinque port of Dover in 1260. The Cinque ports acted as a defence organisation before England had an official navy. In return for this service they received special privileges.

Over the centuries, a number of famous ships sailed out of this North Kent port to fight for this country. One of the most notable was the *Hazard*, which fought in the Armada in 1580. By the wharf in Conduit Street is the Sea Cadets HQ named after it. This beautifully preserved warehouse is even more venerable, dating from the late 1400s.

Shallow-bottomed sailing barges were the most suitable craft to negotiate the tidal waters of the Thames Estuary. They transported heavy bulk cargoes of grain, bricks or cement. Often they were made near their customer's port of usage. Faversham was no exception and one of its greatest exponents of this skilled trade was John Goldfinch. His work was highly regarded and over a long career he produced at least thirty barges. Most weighed around 90 tons, but his final project was a magnificent boat of 144 tons called *Goldfinch*. It was so well designed and constructed that it had a lifespan of fifty-five years and even successfully braved an Atlantic crossing.

Later, during the twentieth century James Pollock & Sons became the town's most significant shipbuilder. From making barges for the Admiralty at their outset in 1875 they grew into a firm capable of putting together coastal vessels of up to 750 tons. However, due to the narrowness of the creek they had to be launched sideways. Output peaked during the Second World War crisis and gradually declined before closure in 1969.

Presently a number of boat repairers ply their trade in workshops along the creek. Near Standard Quay are Peter Dodds, Alan Reekie and Jim Reed. Further downstream at the mouth of the creek where it divides there are well-established traditional wooden boat maintenance facilities. They are adjacent to the Shipwrights Arms where thirsty craftsmen and sailors can handily refresh themselves.

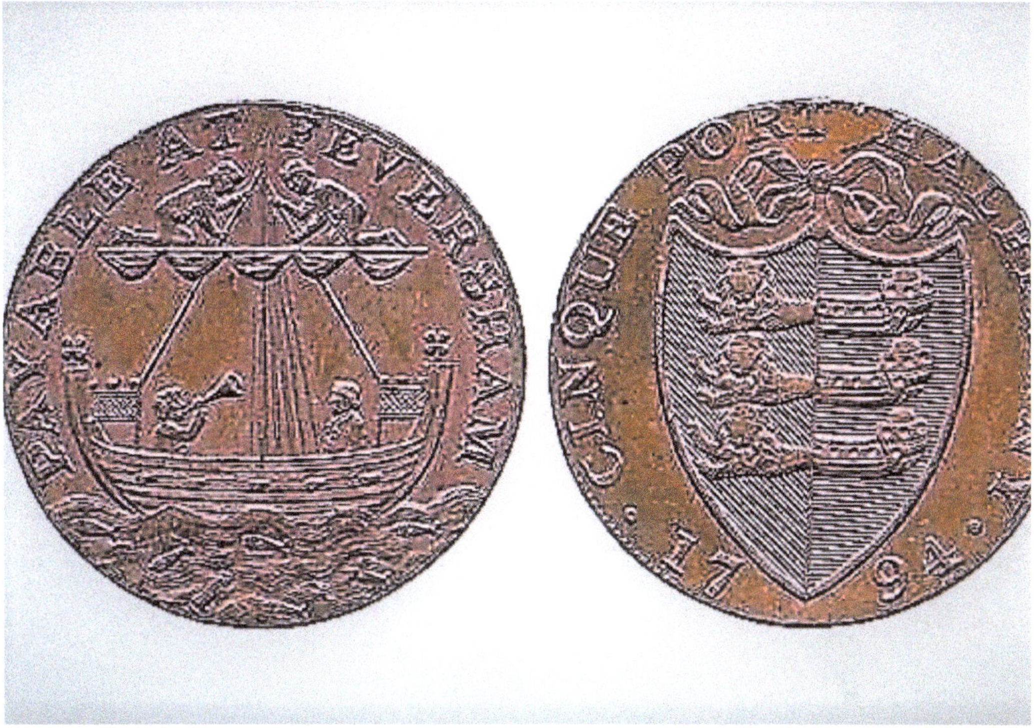

Eighteenth-century trade token depicting Faversham's maritime connections.

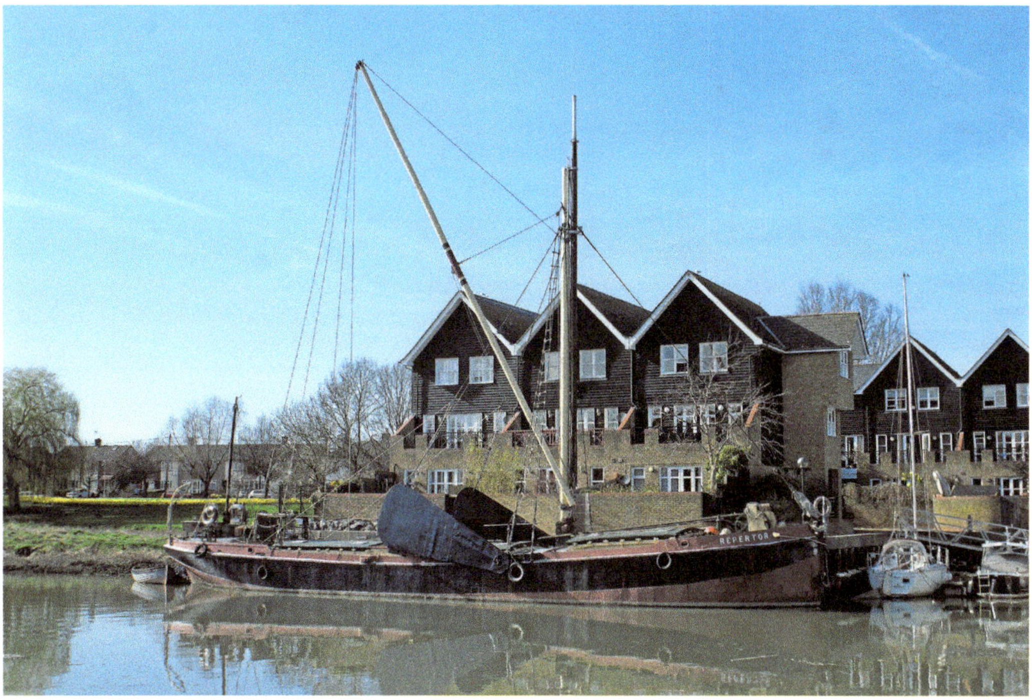

Thames sailing barge docked at the Brents.

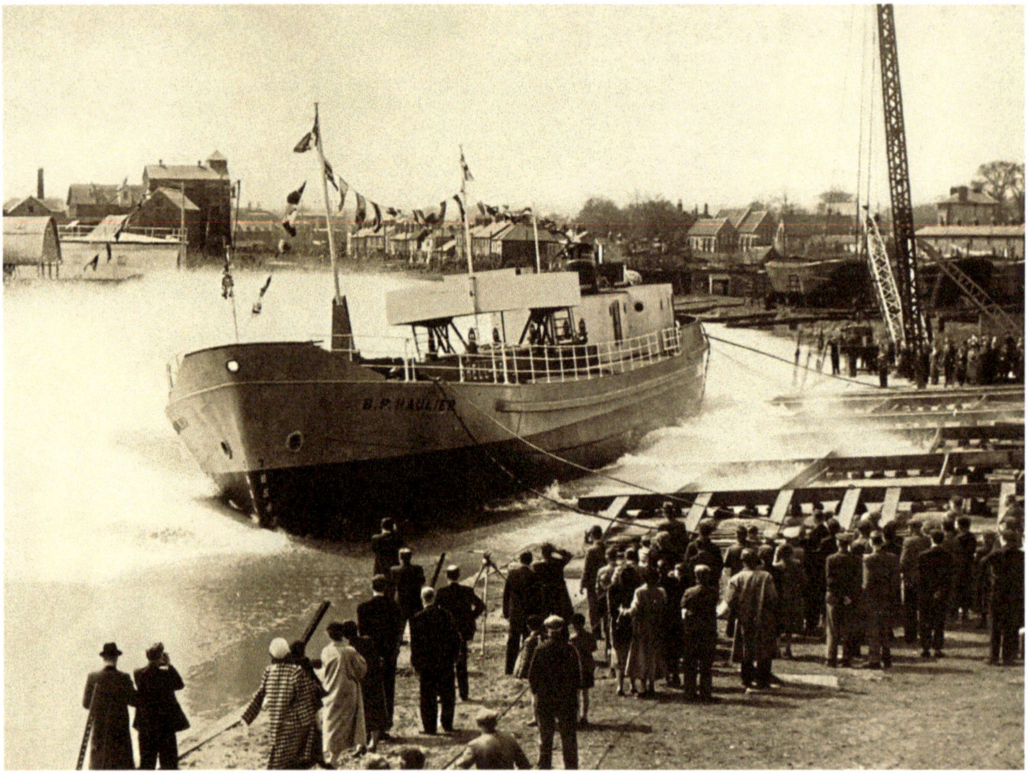

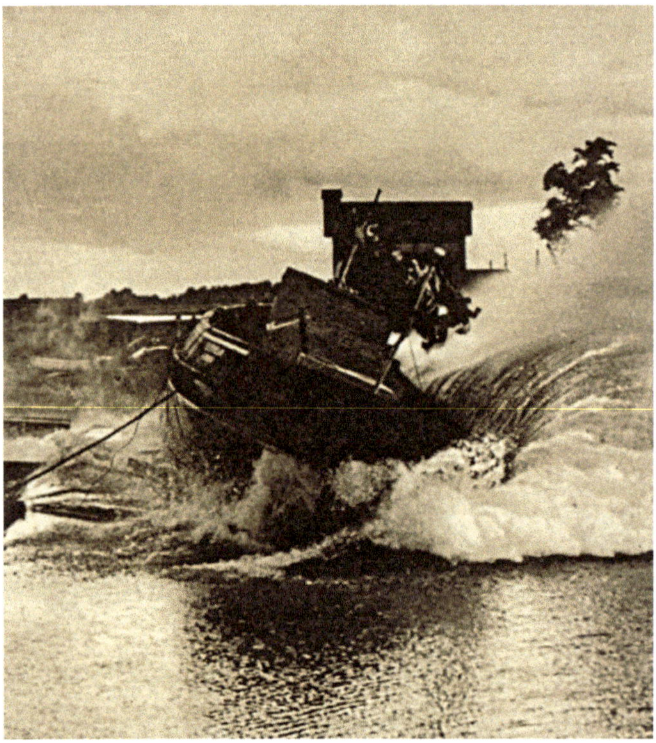

Above: Shipbuilders watching partly completed project.

Left: More dramatic illustration of sideways launching method.

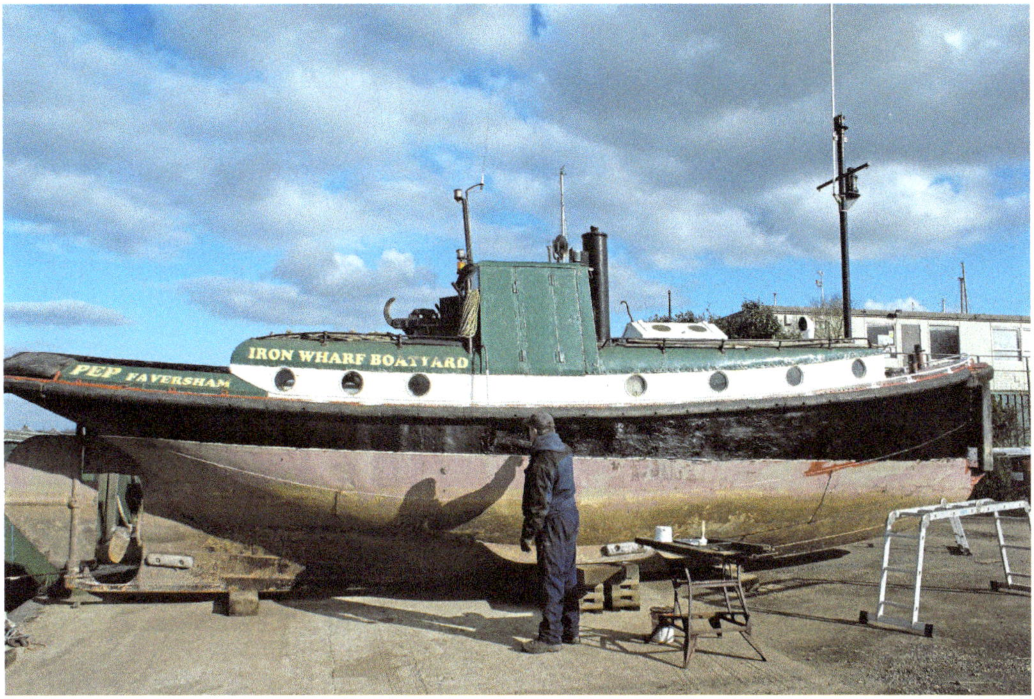

Present-day boat repairer.

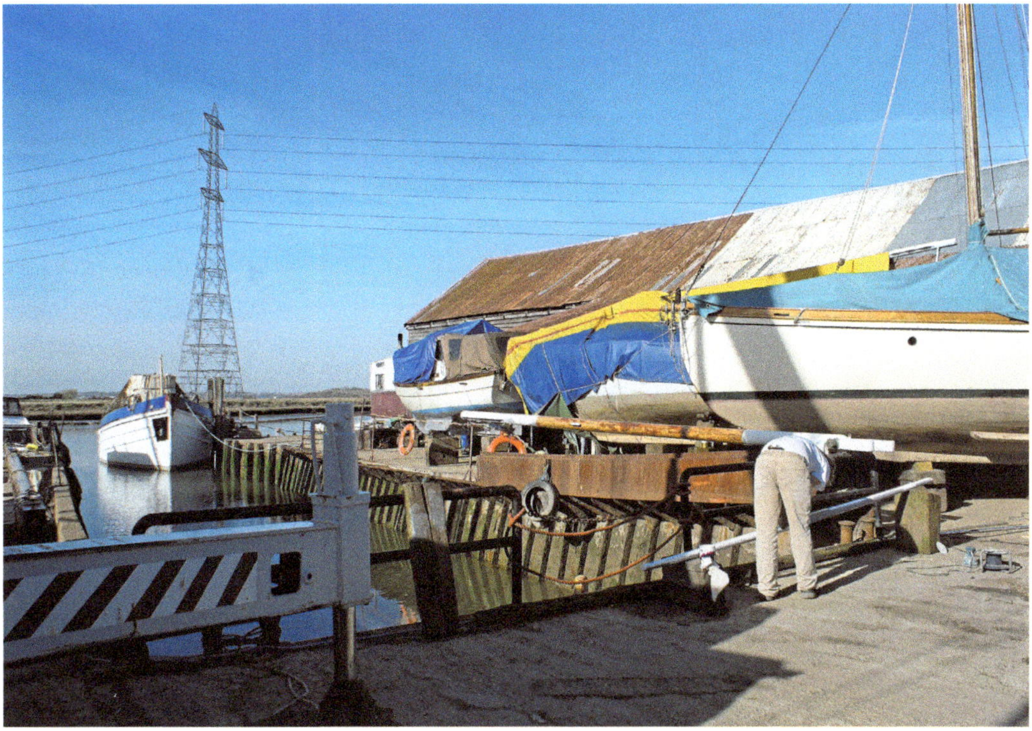

Dock at Hollowshore.

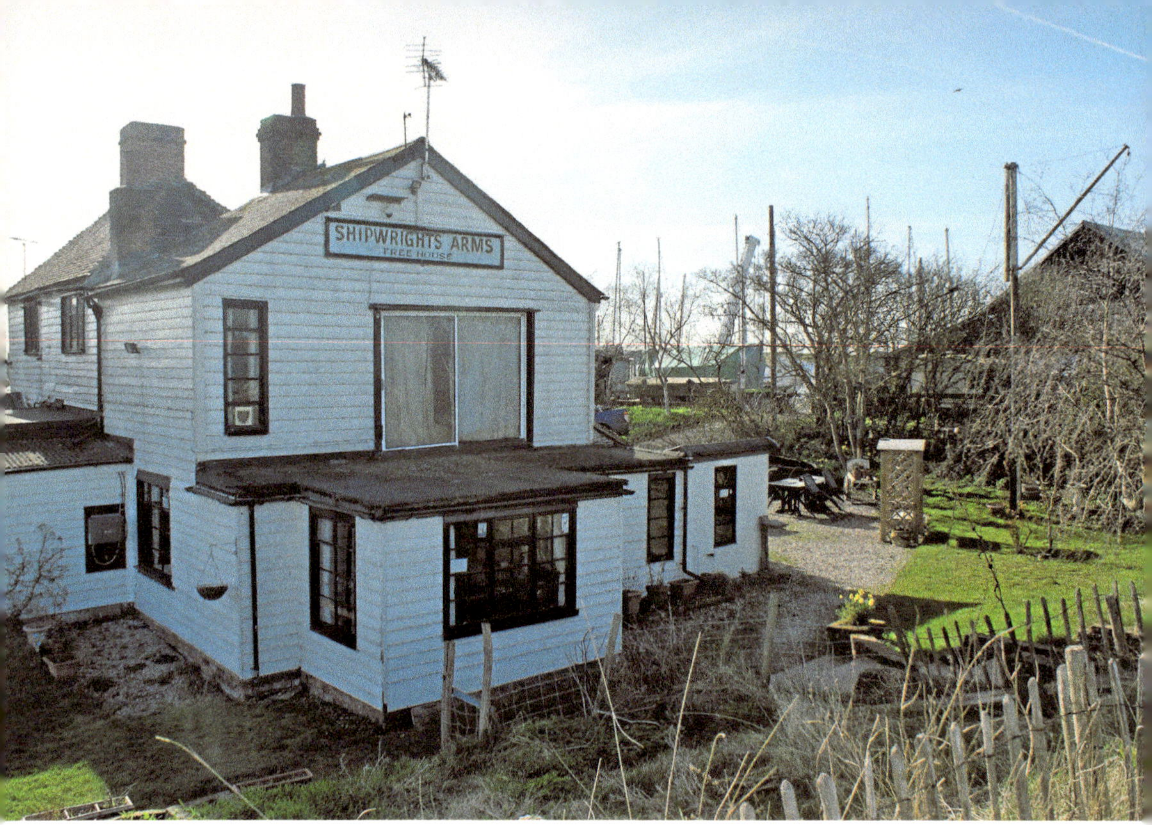

Above: The Shipwrights Arms.

Below: Hollowshore Boatyard.

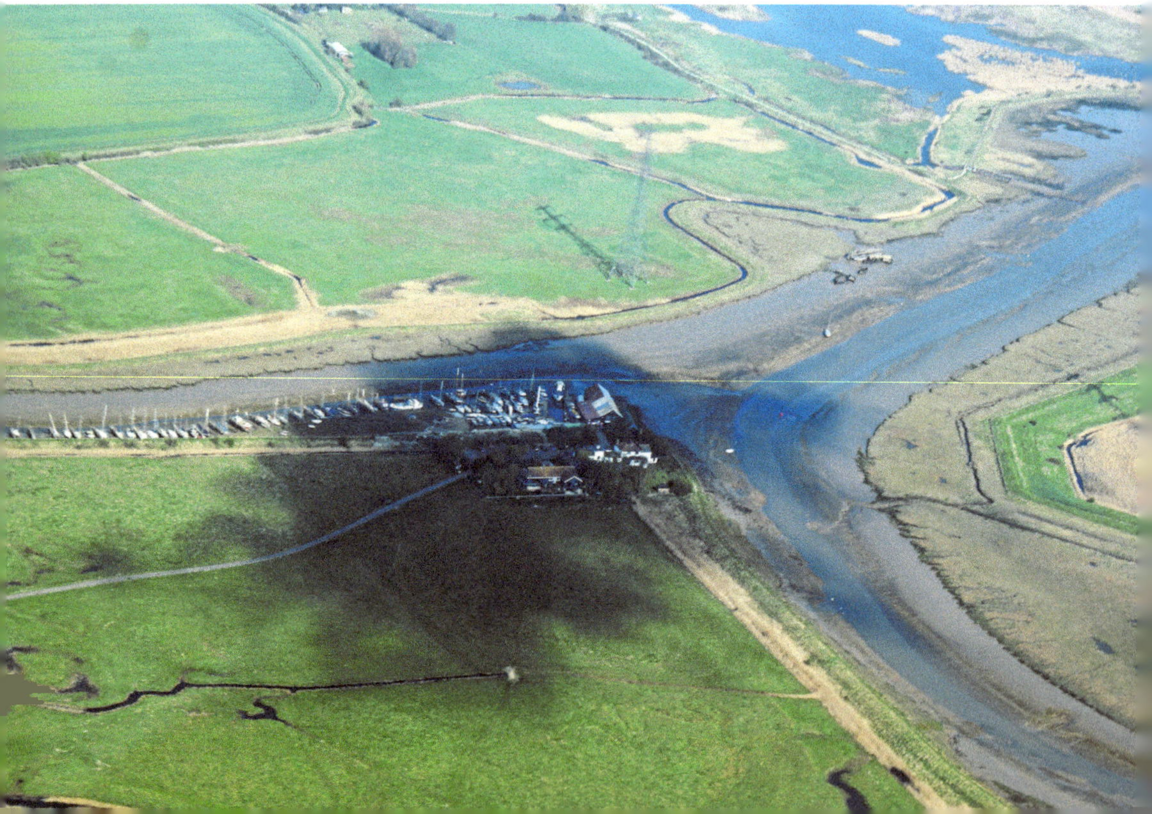

FARMING

'Kent, sir everybody knows Kent - apples, cherries, hops and women.' Thus Charles Dickens described the Garden of England in *The Pickwick Papers*. Faversham is placed right in the centre of North Kent's horticultural belt.

Brogdale is the home of the largest collection of fruit varieties in the world. They are planted in 150 acres of orchards, which are open to the public. Scientific responsibility for them is under the curation of Reading University, who conduct research and maintain this genetic source. Trees are available to buy, but other niche businesses such as a microbrewery and a butcher can be found on site.

The introduction of cherries to England by Henry VIII's fruiterer was at the next settlement west of Faversham – Teynham. It is not surprising that over subsequent centuries this area became engulfed in orchards. Growing conditions are ideal. Soil quality is good – more often the relatively rare Grade 1 category. Whereas, a favourably mild temperate climate is of great assistance also.

Previously orchards had low-density, high or 'standard' tree trunks. These required tall ladders for pickers to reach the highest fruits. Now plantations comprise much smaller low pruned trees where crops can be gathered at ground level. The old and present-day methods can be compared from the following illustrations. Also the modern, prevalent, use of metal hoops to support a protective tunnel can be observed.

Hops were first imported to Faversham to make beer for Low Country immigrants. However, sometime in the sixteenth century they started to be planted locally in rich fertile brick earth. Slowly during the 1700s this specialist crop gained popularity among nearby farmers keen to supply the town's breweries. In particular, the Neame family were prominent in both activities.

By Victorian times it had become a massive industry with 80,000 seasonal workers from London arriving in Kent. They were joined by gypsies who had finished fruit picking. All lived in crude accommodation – either caravans or huts. Sometimes there were clashes between cockneys and country folk, but for most it was treated as a holiday in fresh air with the benefit of pay. Mechanisation has displaced this army of workers and any casual labour now needed is often provided by energetic Eastern Europeans.

Each year Faversham celebrates its old customs with a very popular street fair called the Hop Festival, where much music and drink encourages jollity.

Although agriculturally renowned for fruit and hops in particular, other branches of farming are easily pursued because of excellent conditions. Vast areas of arable are planted. Their cultivation has become dependent on huge technologically advanced implements such as the gargantuan

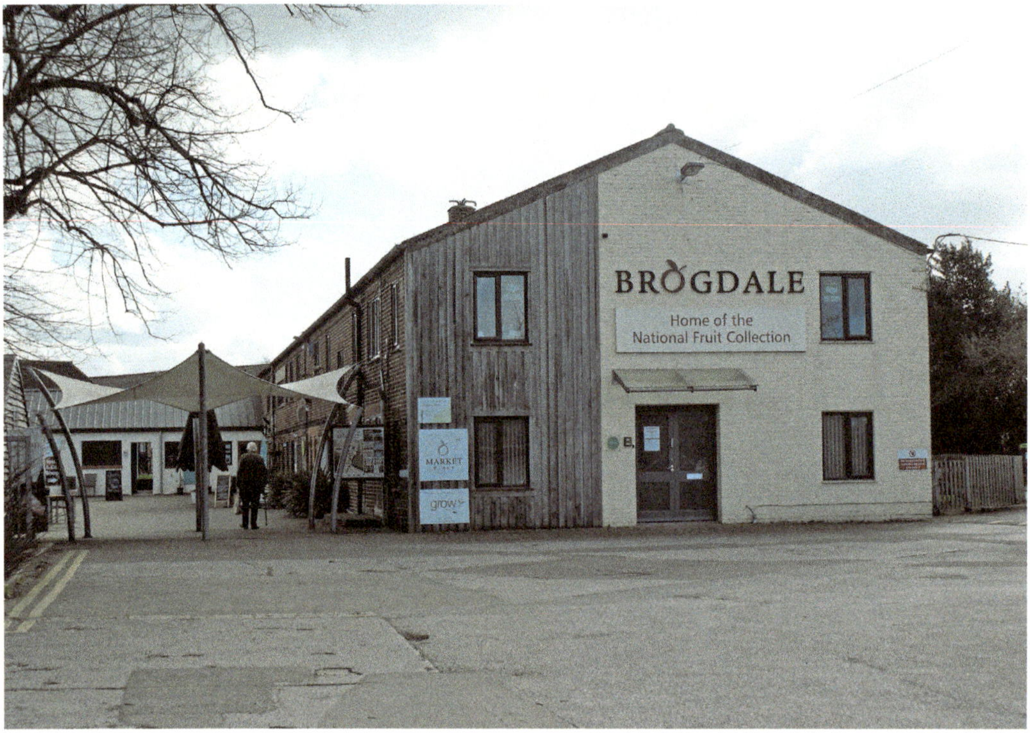

Brogdale Visitor Centre.

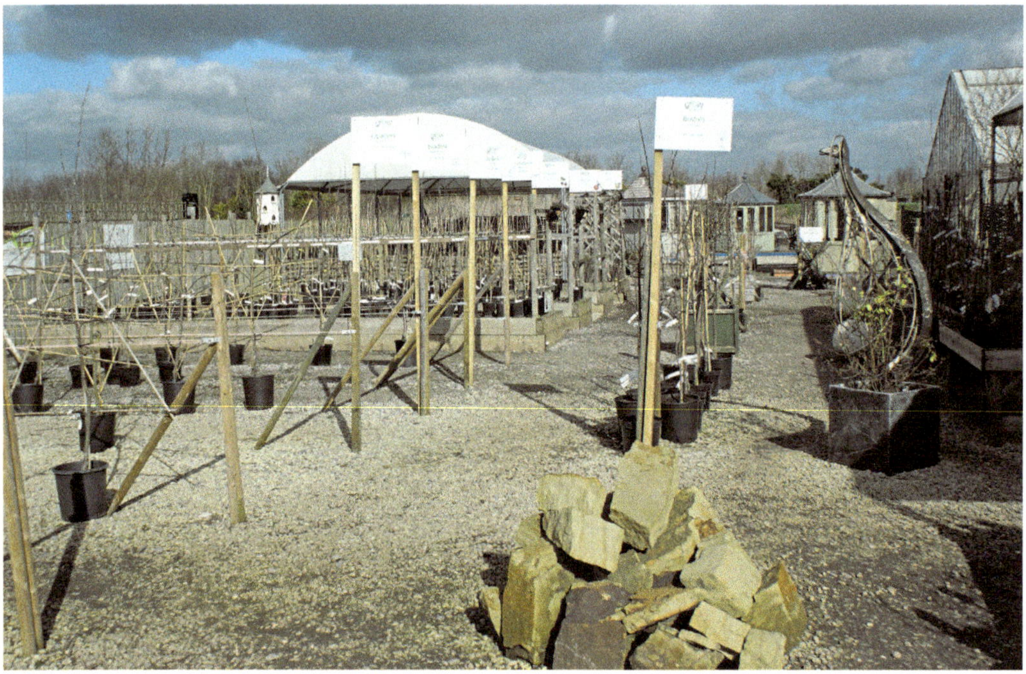

Fruit trees for sale to the public.

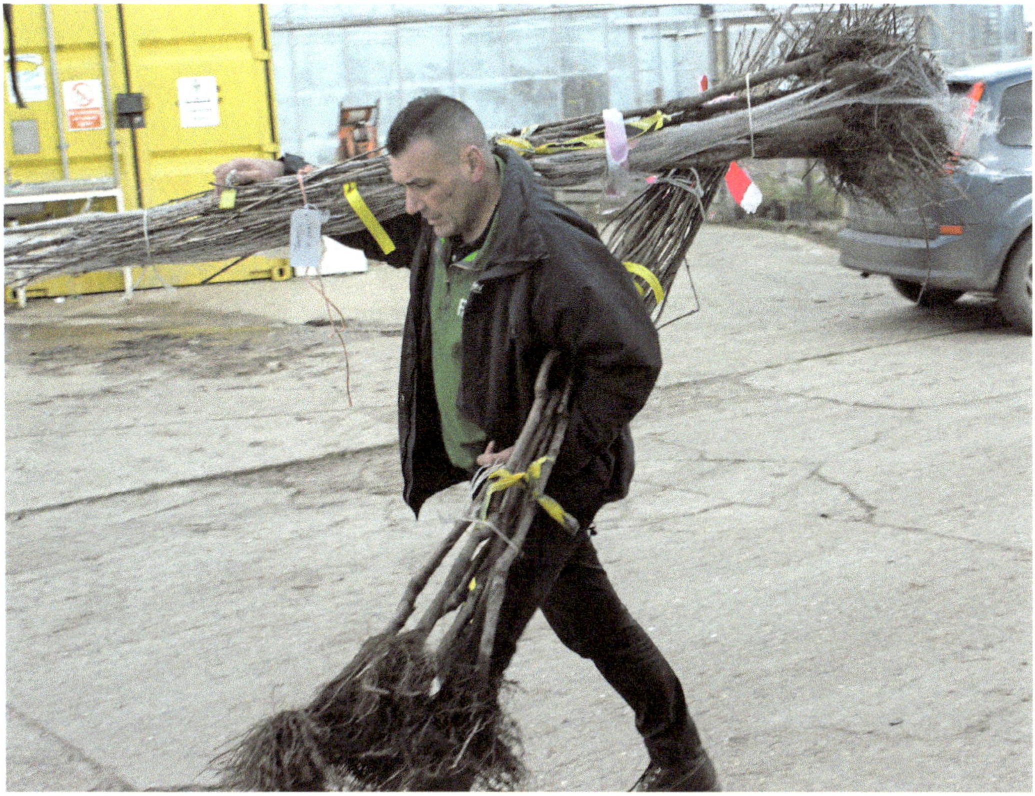

Fruit trees before transplantation.

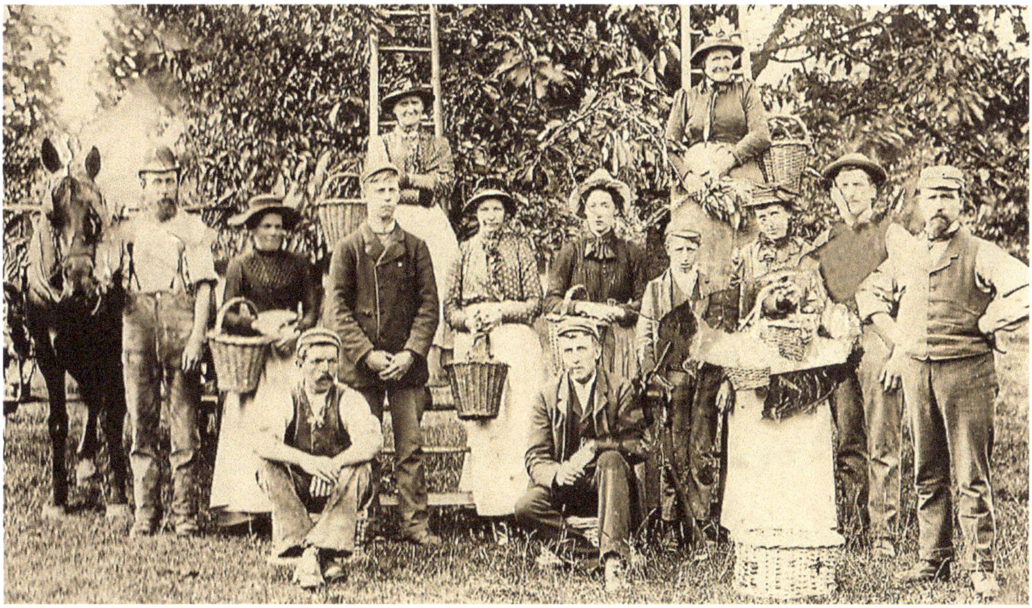

Victorian cherry pickers.

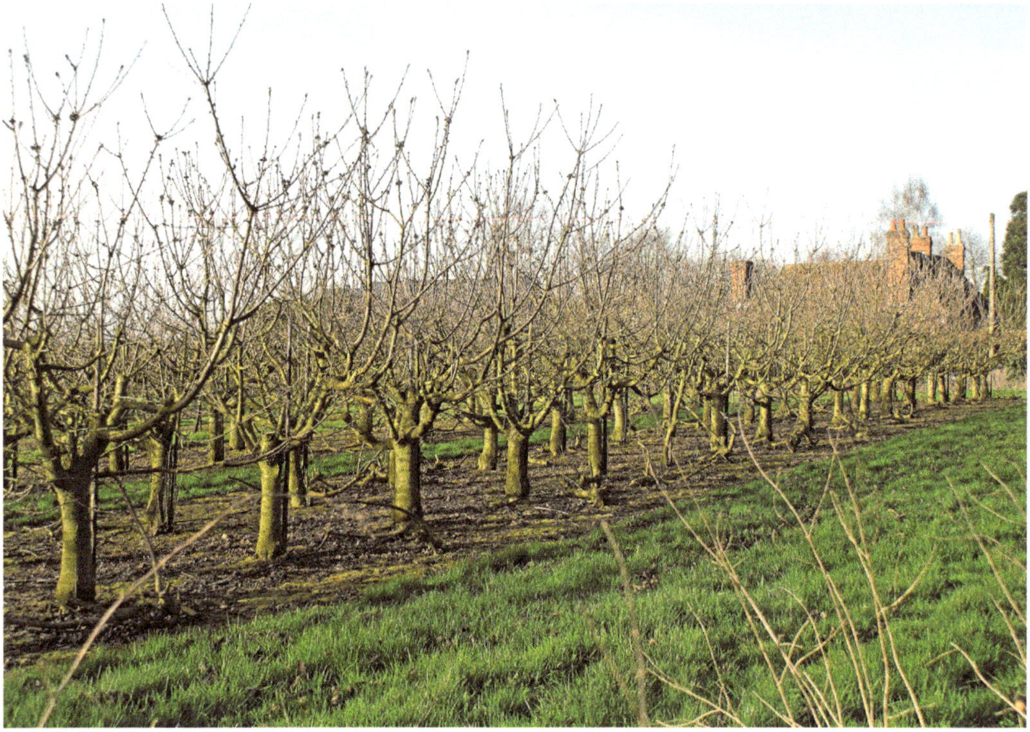

Two-row bed apple production technique.

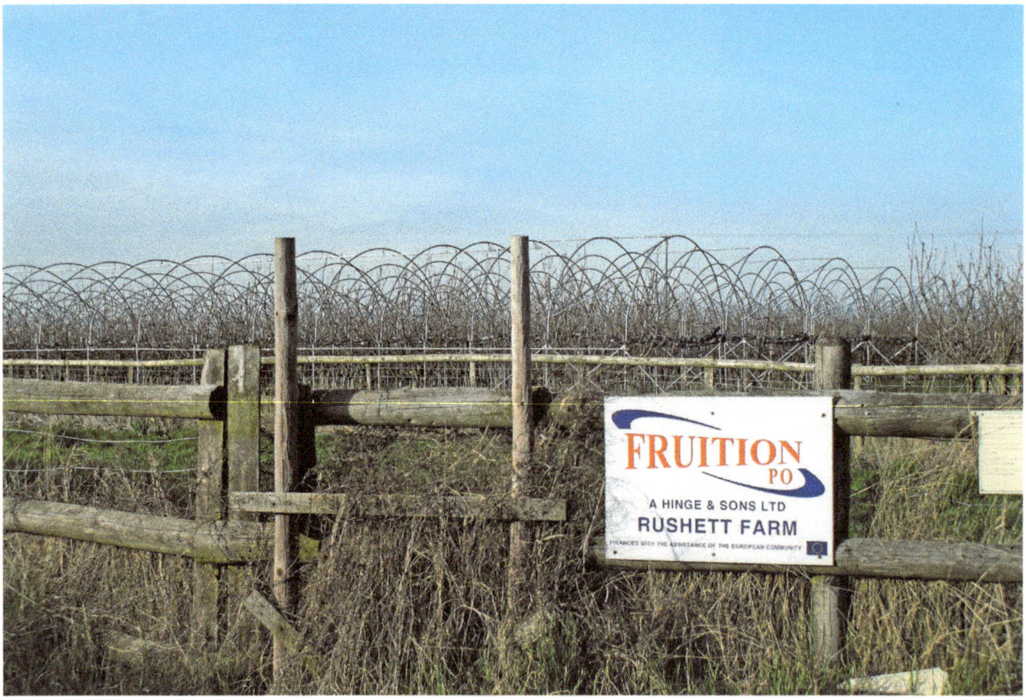

Metal frames to support protective tunnels over cherry trees.

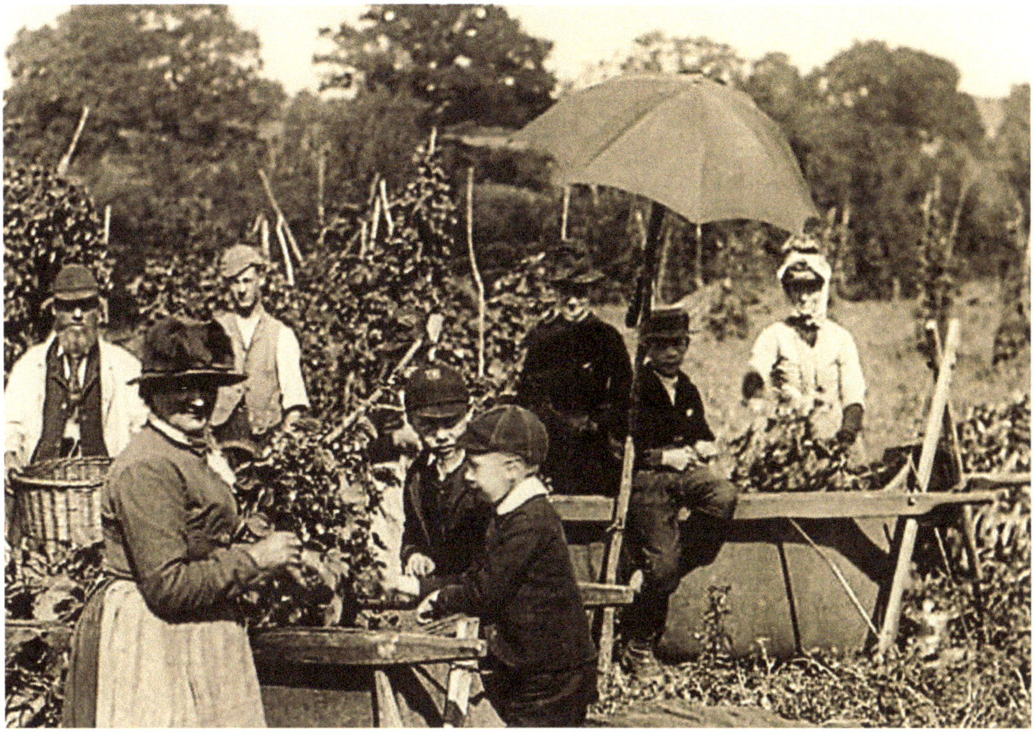

Victorian labourers stripping hop bines of their vital flowers.

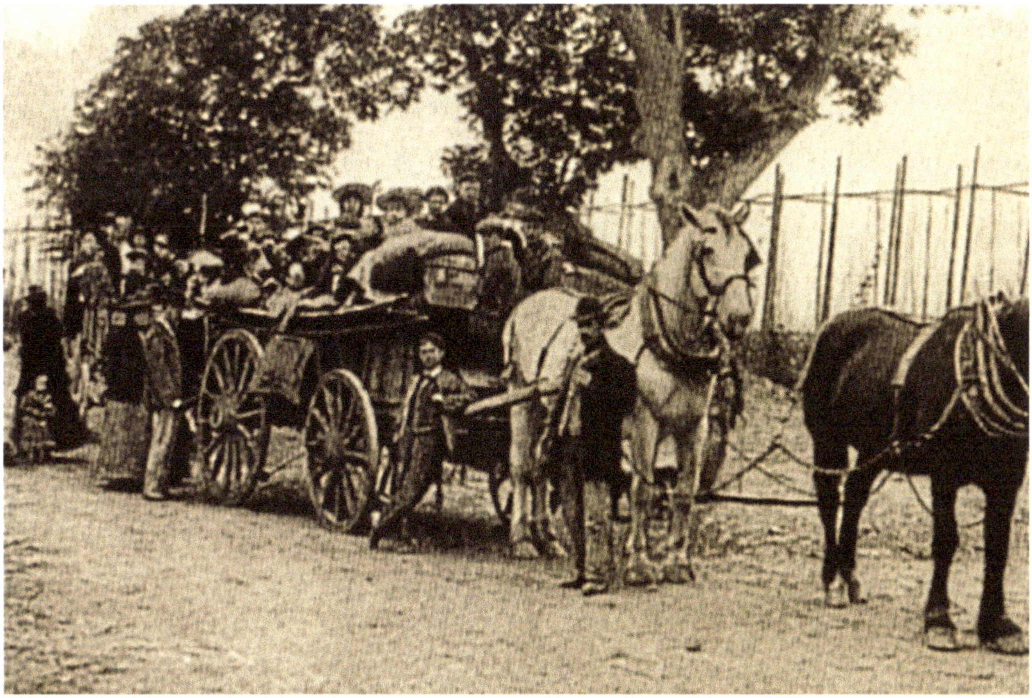

Hop pickers arriving with their belongings for the seasonal work stay.

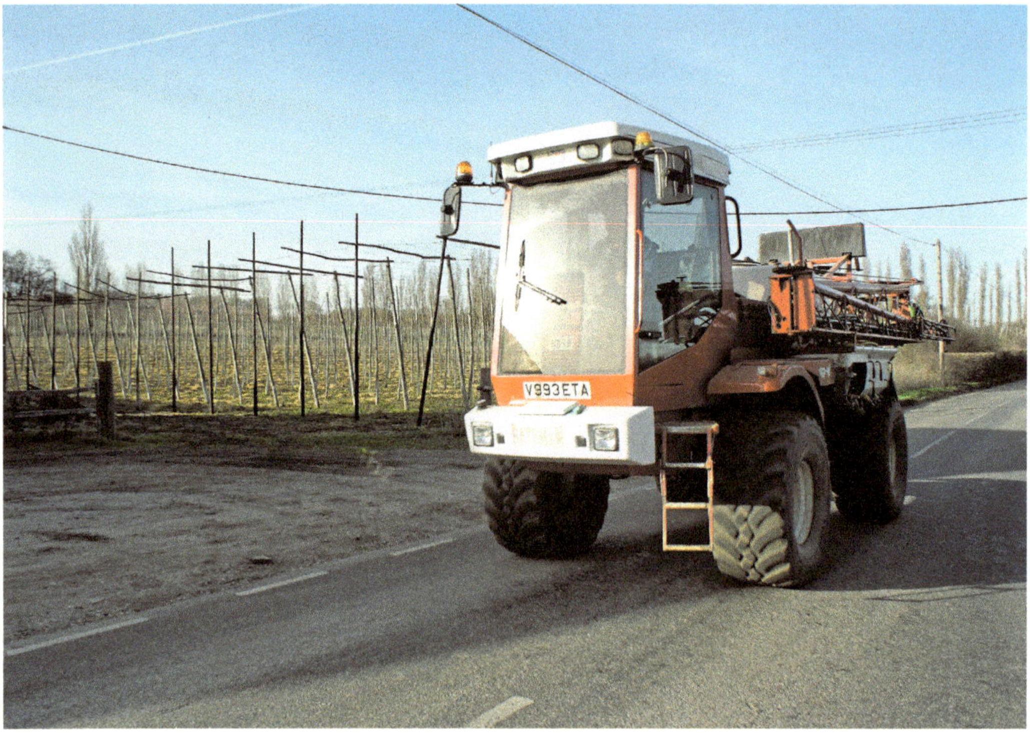

Modern arable crop sprayer in Newnham Valley.

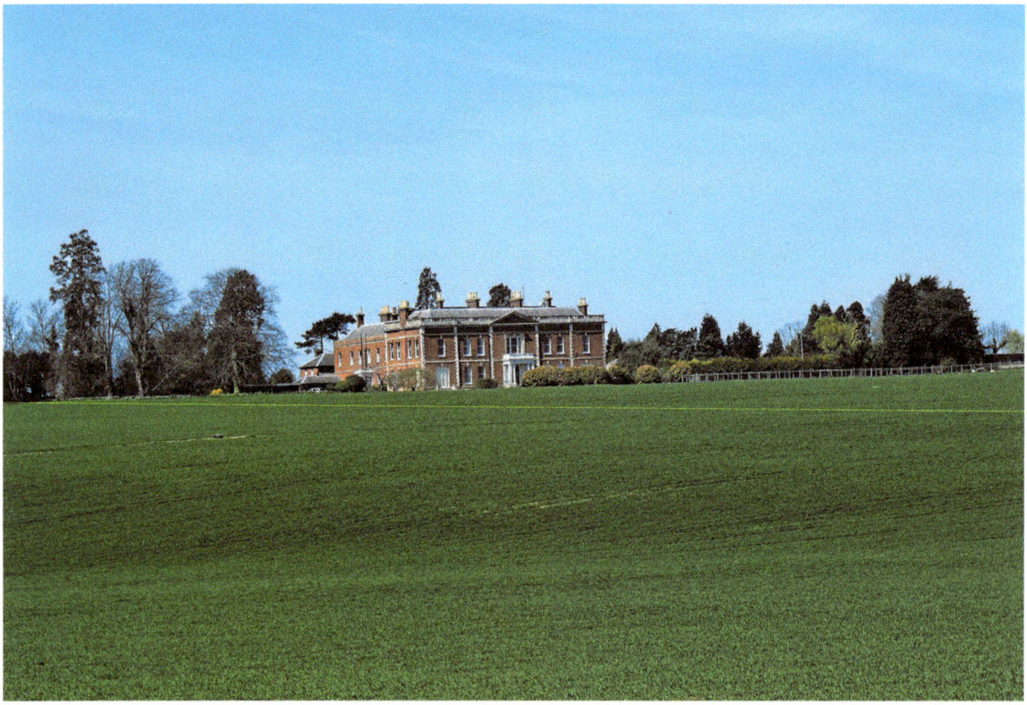

Extensive corn fields near Faversham.

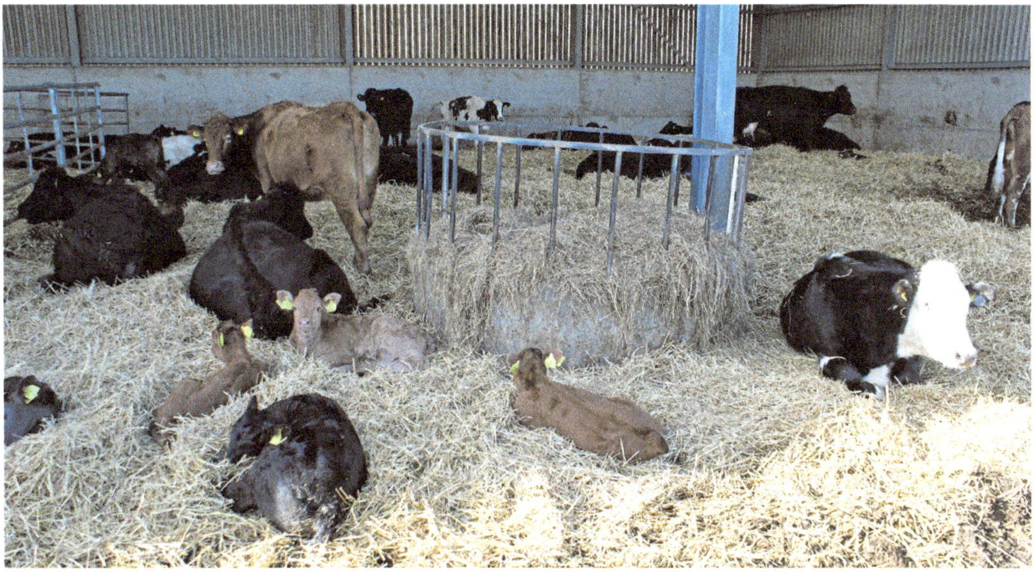

Young calves at Ham Farm.

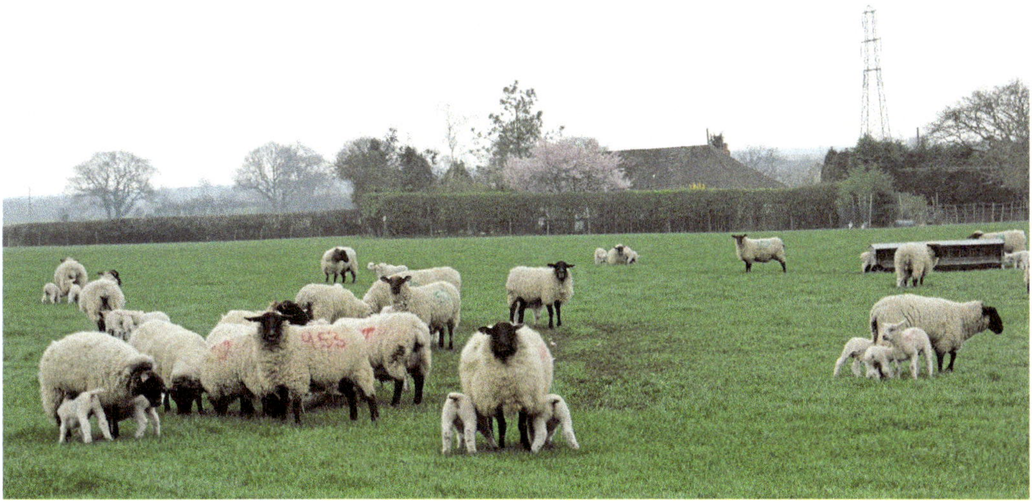

Breading a flock of sheep on North Downs.

sprayer pictured earlier. Capital plants like this can require investment sums of upwards of £70,000! Even more expensive are combine harvesters frequently costing £250,000.

Also outstanding animal husbandry is practised on specialist farms more suited for this. To the north, on Ham marshes, the Bray family are heavily engaged in cattle breading. On rising ground southwards, sheep farming is more likely to prosper.

From these observations, the present state of agriculture here is most healthy. But it is based upon long-held traditions. Faversham was in Tudor times this country's largest exporter of wool. Much of the nation's wealth and future comparative economic strength was derived from this trade. Grain was another important source of revenue with large volumes leaving as cargoes bound for London.

SHOPS AND RESTAURANTS

Around its historic town hall Faversham holds street markets three days per week. It is the oldest market in Kent and the right to hold it is enshrined in ancient charters. In fact, this town owns one of the country's finest collections of municipal charters. Among these treasures is a copy of the Magna Carta dated 1300. To illustrate and explain these valuable documents the much admired and revered Faversham Society has published a lavish volume about them by Dr Arthur Percival MBE, FSA.

Presently, the colourful stalls offer an array of local produce including fruit and vegetables. New-laid eggs, flowers, bread, cheese and game are also available. Craft baker James of Wild Bread is pictured on page 51 sampling one of his handmade sour dough loaves.

Antiques and other collectibles can be rummaged through on different stalls. One trader has a particularly fine display of old earthenware bottles and flagons on offer. Once a month there is a larger street antiques' market (the only one known in this country). At this venue larger items including furniture can be purchased.

Ever increasingly, this town's reputation for junk and antique shops has grown. Dealers have opened up in a number of streets. Although demand for brown furniture is currently depressed, the traditional denizens of Faversham are at least interested in lighter pine or oak chattels.

In the well-preserved Abbey Warehouse at Standard Quay, fifteen dealers have their operations. This a lovely old timber and brick building, which, among its earlier uses, was a grain mill. On its second floor, Lisa is snapped, on a following page, proudly standing by the entrance. Below, Phil Selby and Sarah Perry of Country Clobber have a fantastic collection of vintage steel tools and forged implements awaiting buyers. Nearby furniture made prior to 1850 is galleried by Medway Antiques.

Adding to the convivial dockside atmosphere there is a café serving light refreshments. Faversham now copies Continental boulevard style with pubs and cafés putting tables and chairs outside on pavements. The intrinsic attractiveness of Faversham makes it a natural tourist destination and for pleasure boat owners a convenient place to sail from.

Walking back from the creek side into Court Street, one comes across lots of interesting specialist shops. One that stands out is the Yarn Dispensary, which occupies premises of a very old chemists. Although only trading from this period shop for less than two years, it is sought after by handcraft knitters who happen to be highly discerning knowledgeable customers.

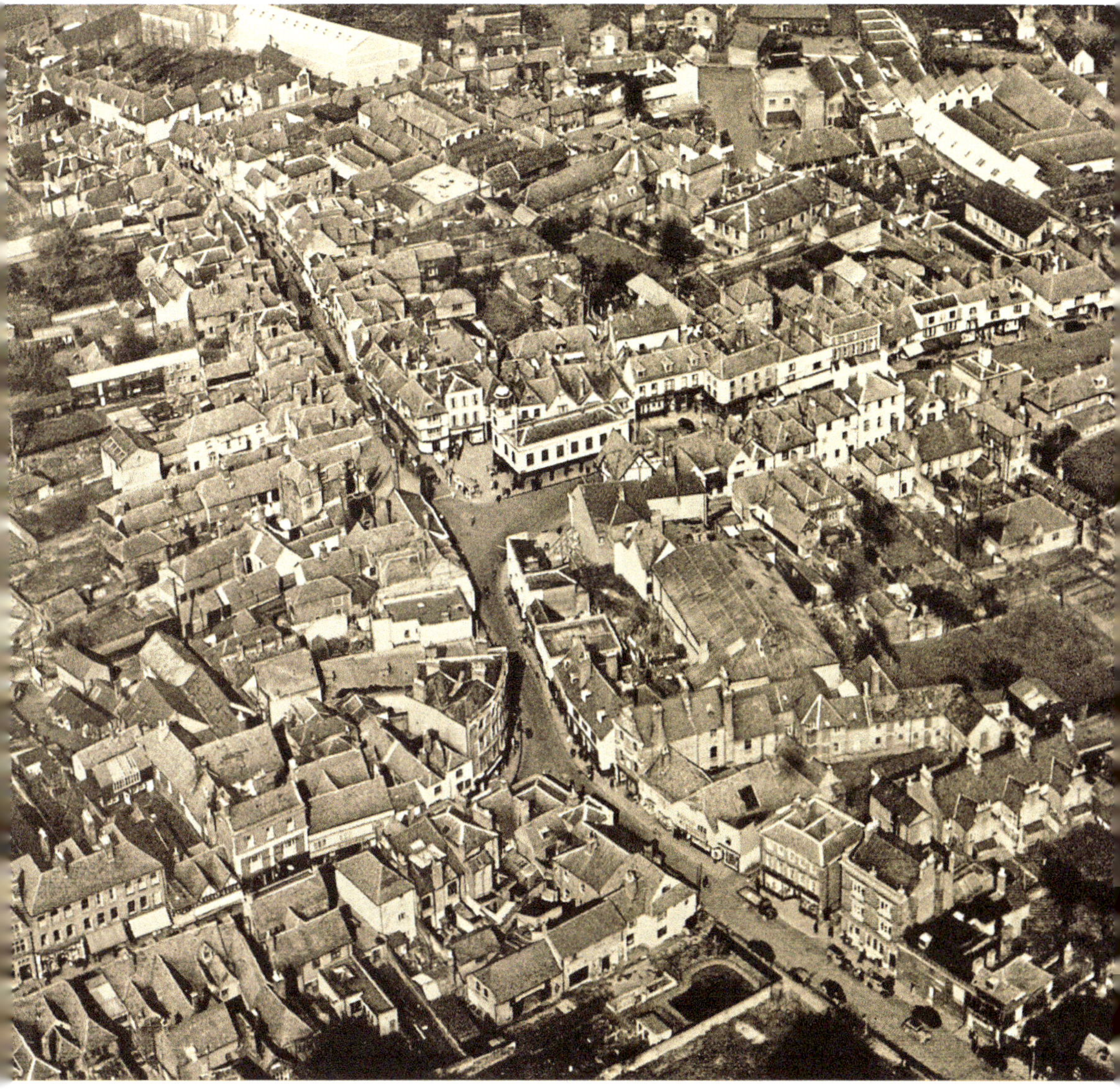

Aerial view of town centre.

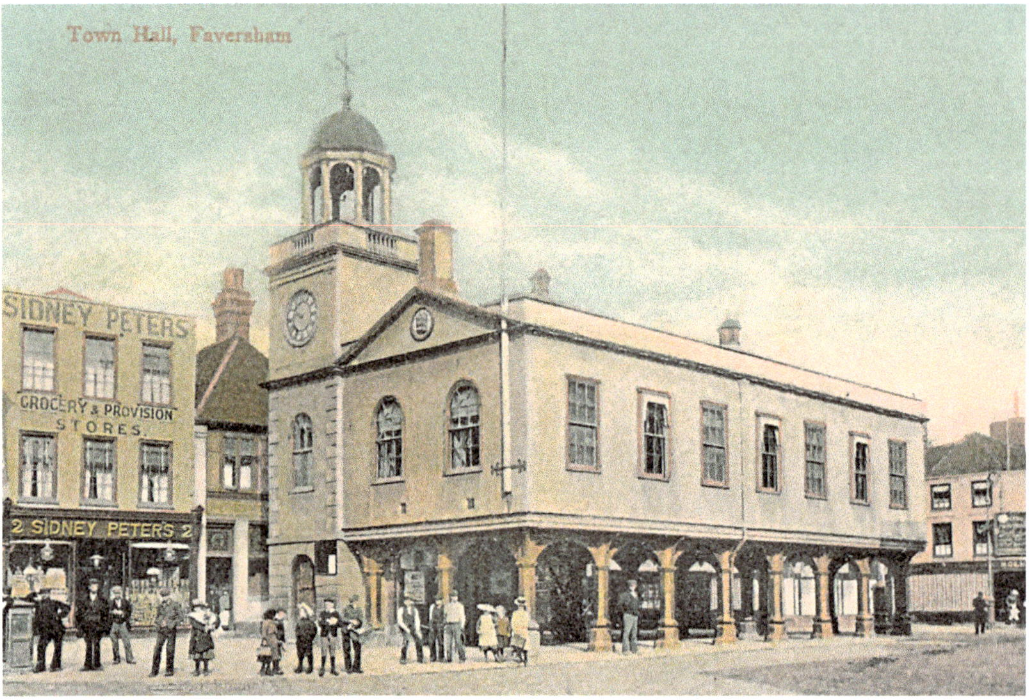

Town Hall image from an Edwardian postcard.

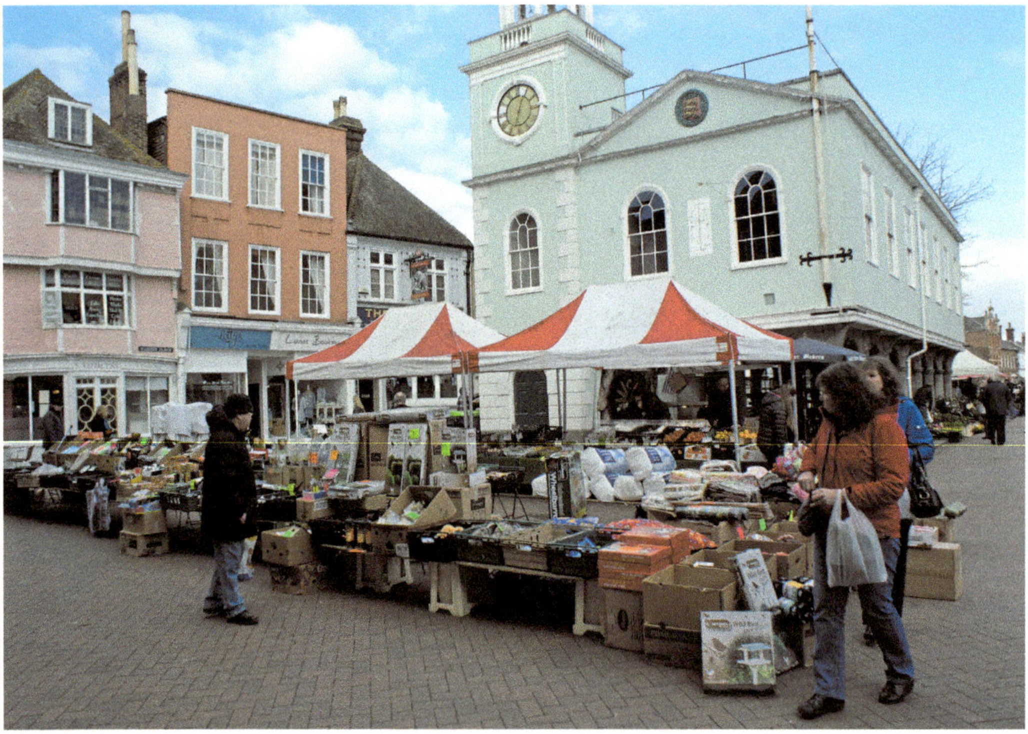

Present-day market stalls.

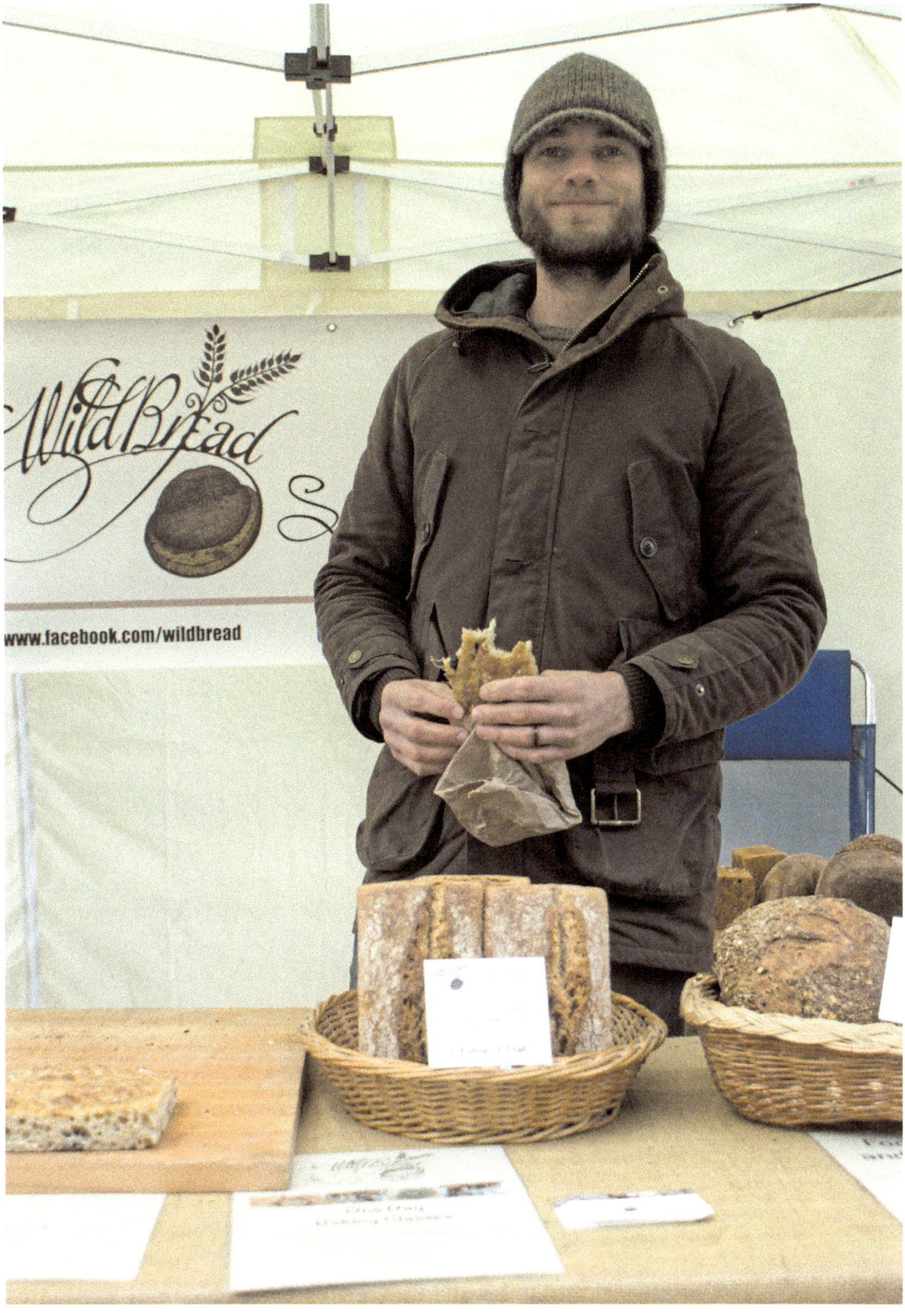

James of Wild Bread, bakers.

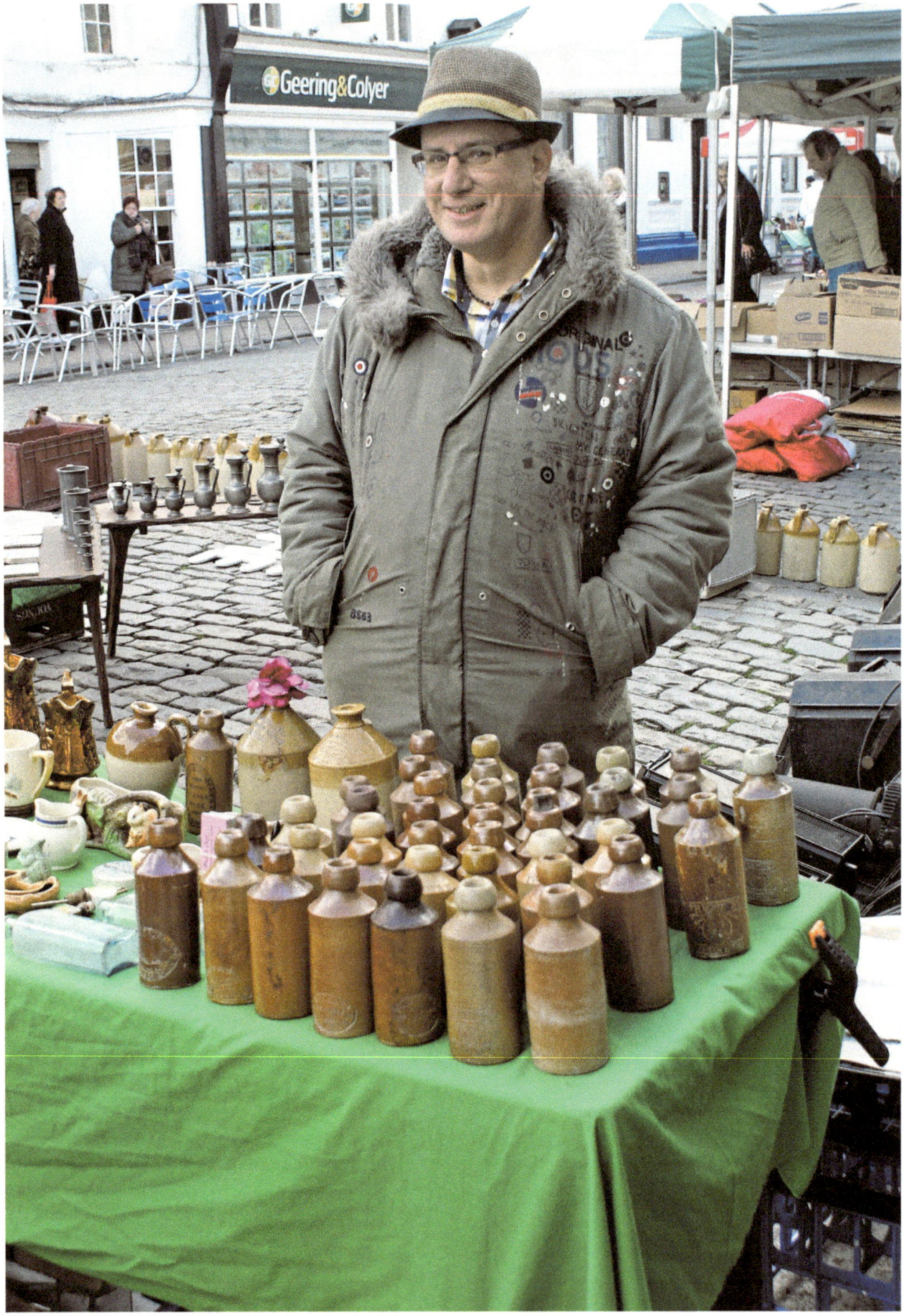

Specialist antique bottle dealer.

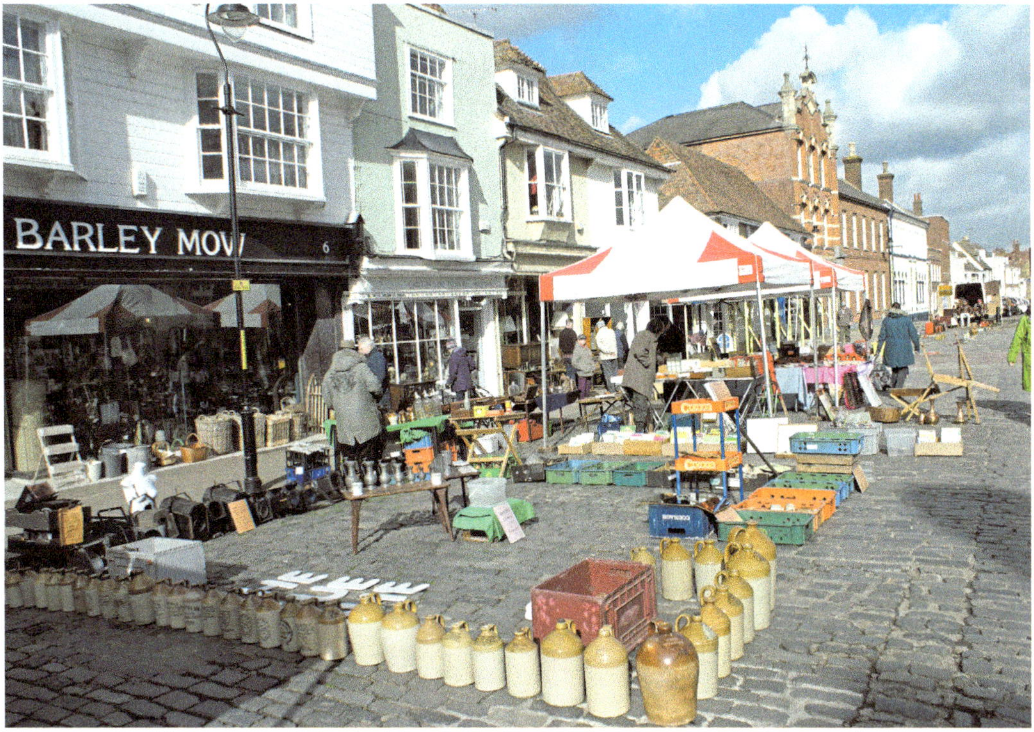

Extensive array of earthenware flagons.

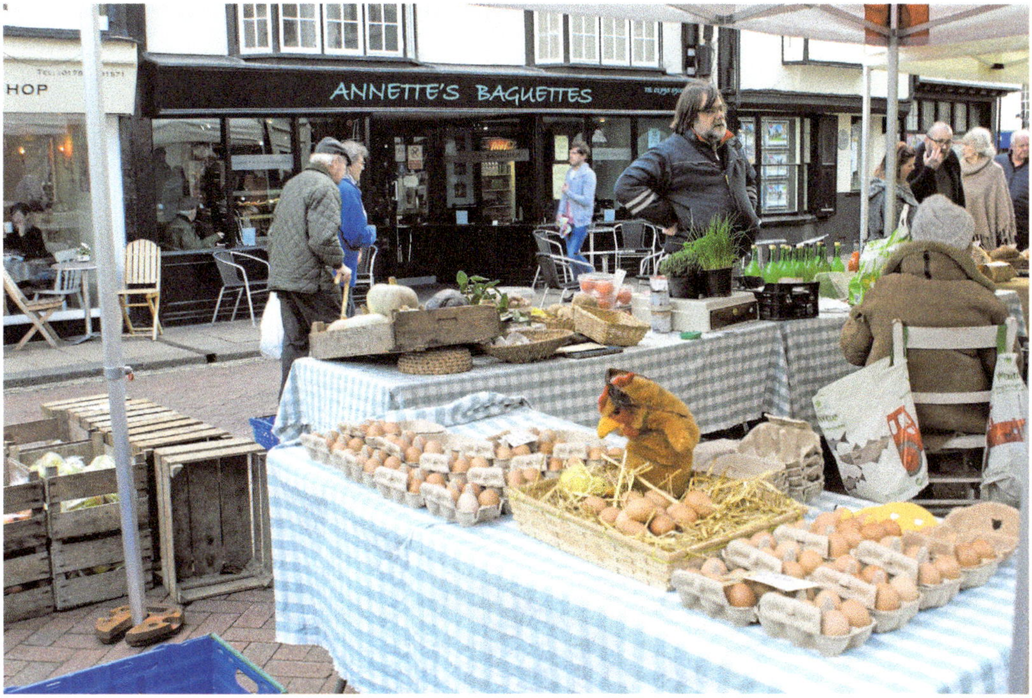

Farm-fresh eggs for sale.

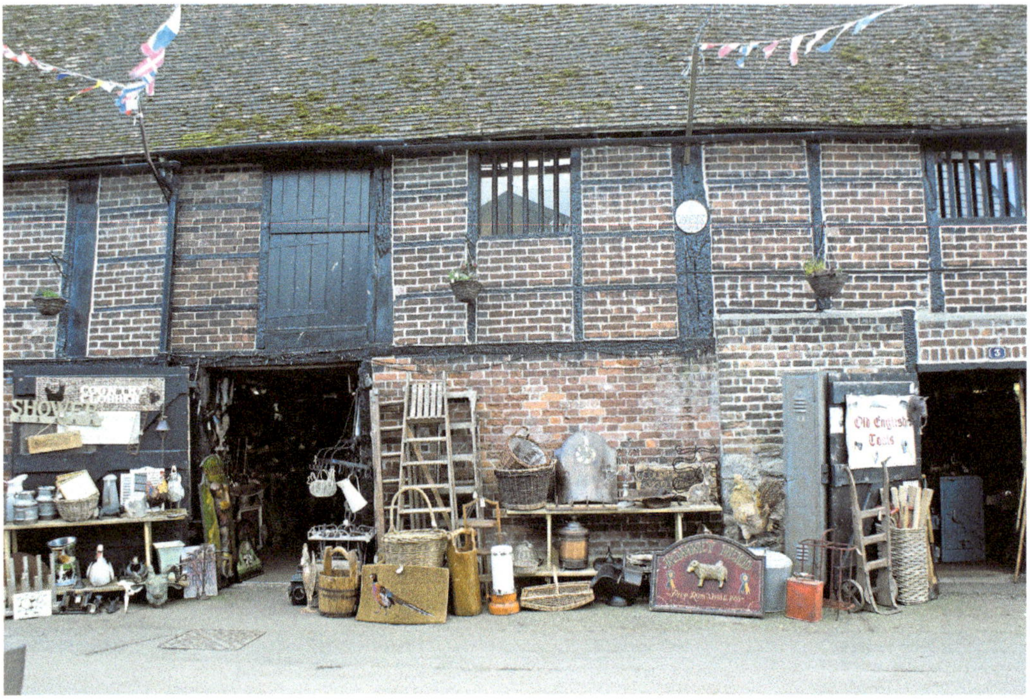

Abbey Warehouse, Standard Quay.

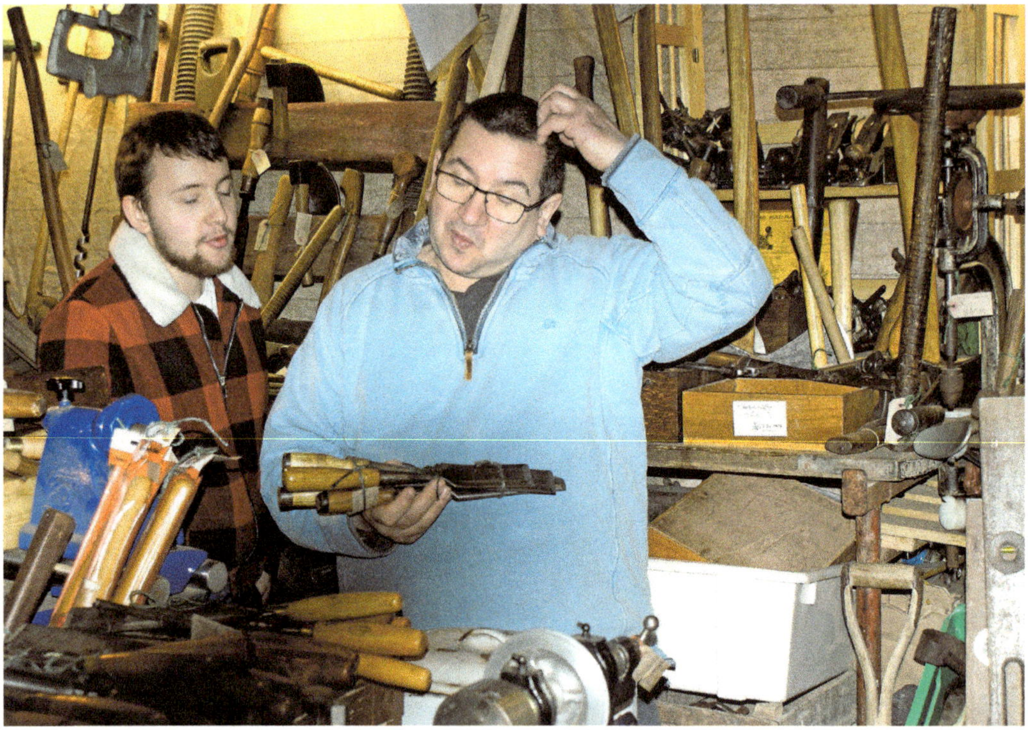

Customers evaluating stock at Country Clobber.

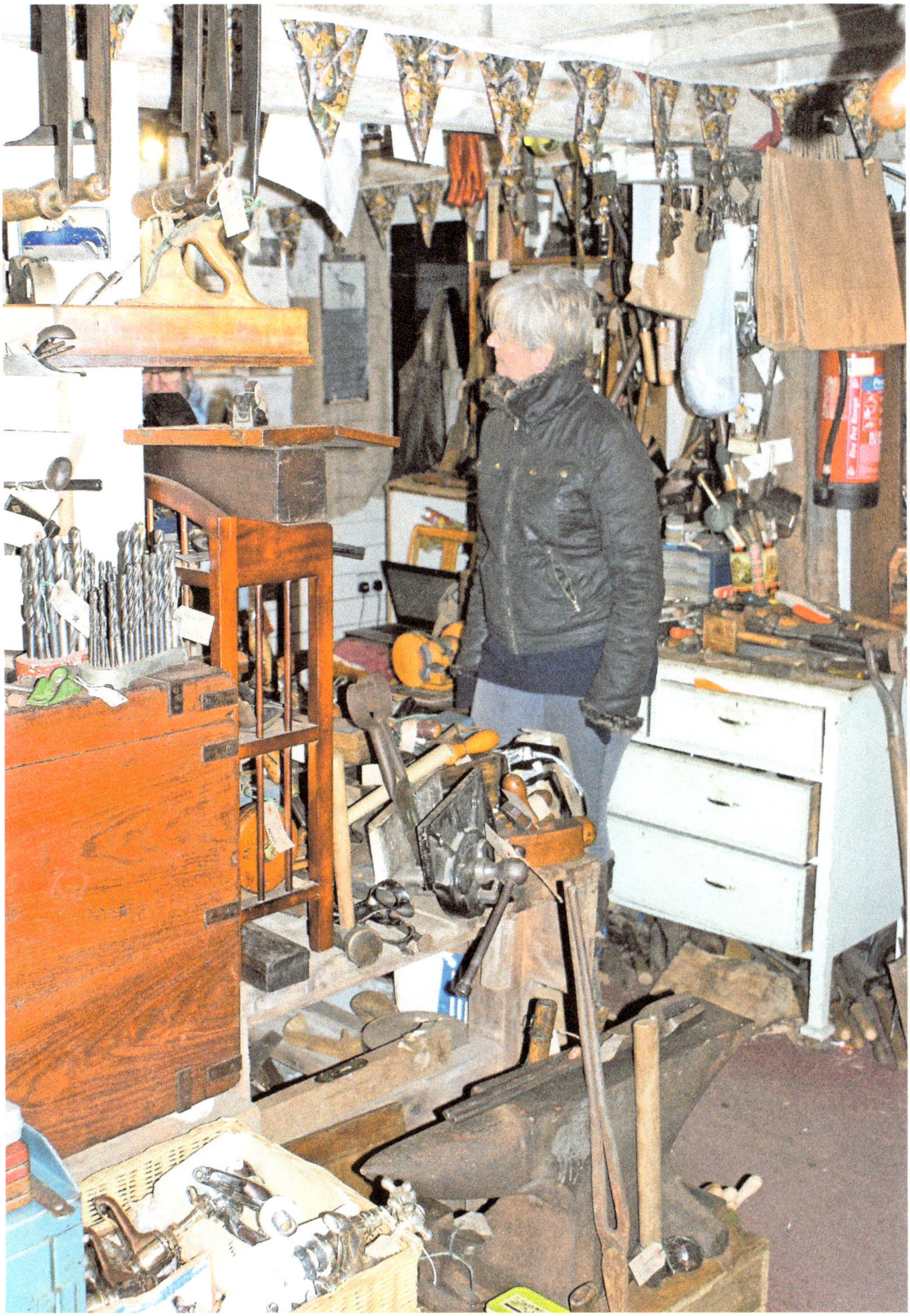

Vintage tools galore at Country Clobber.

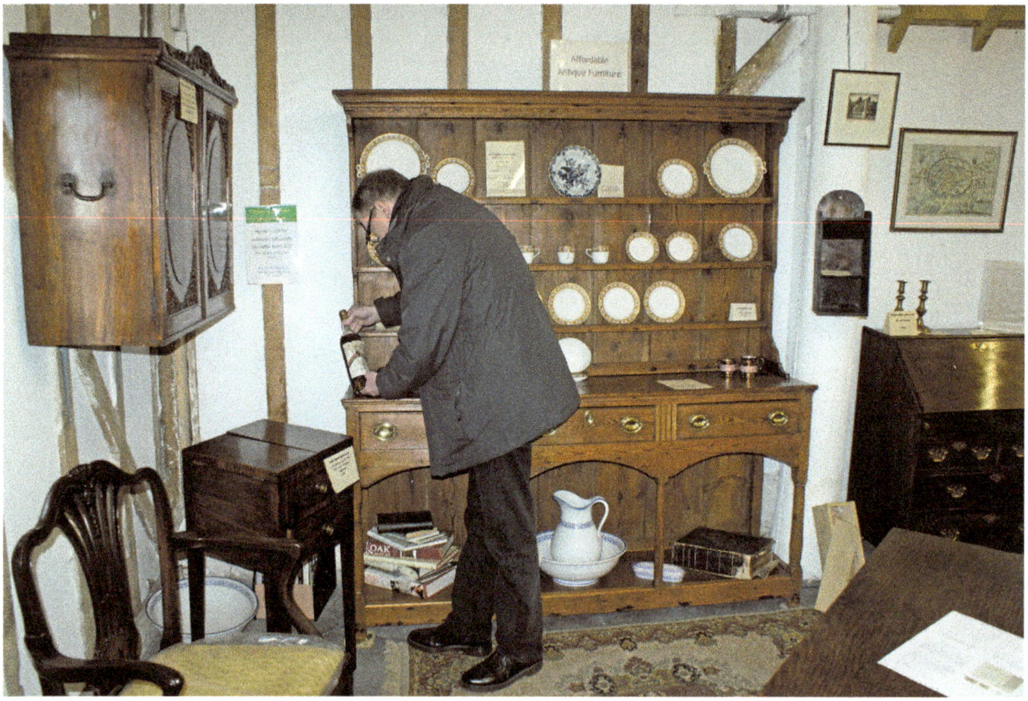

Medway antique's showroom, Standard Quay.

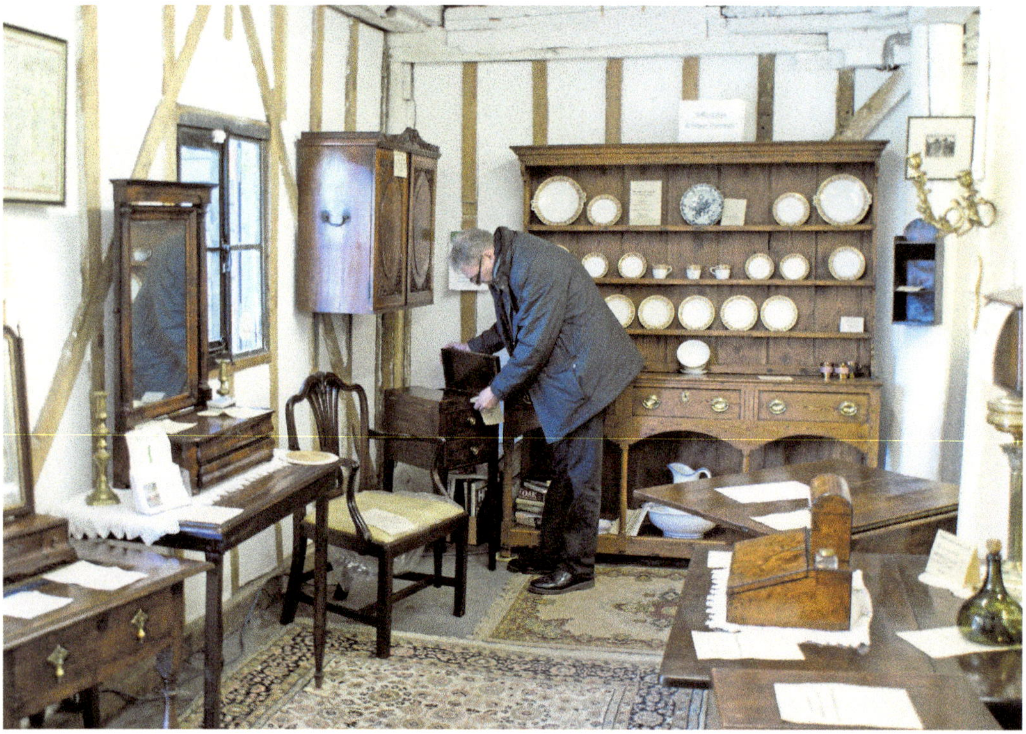

Gallery of furniture made prior to around 1850.

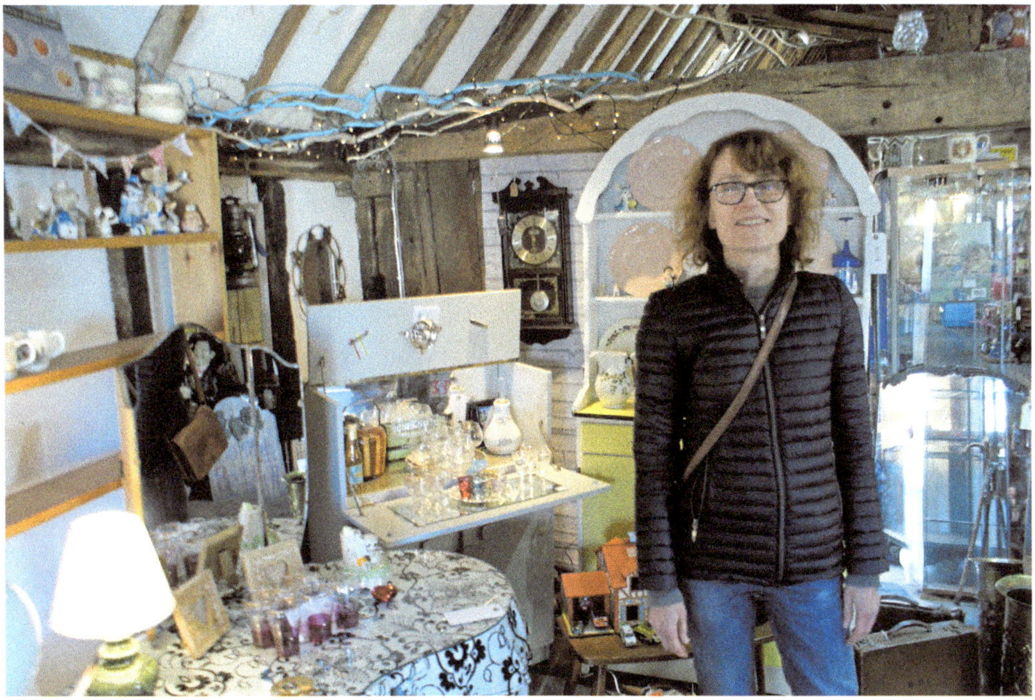

Lisa amid her sale items on the first floor of Abbey Warehouse.

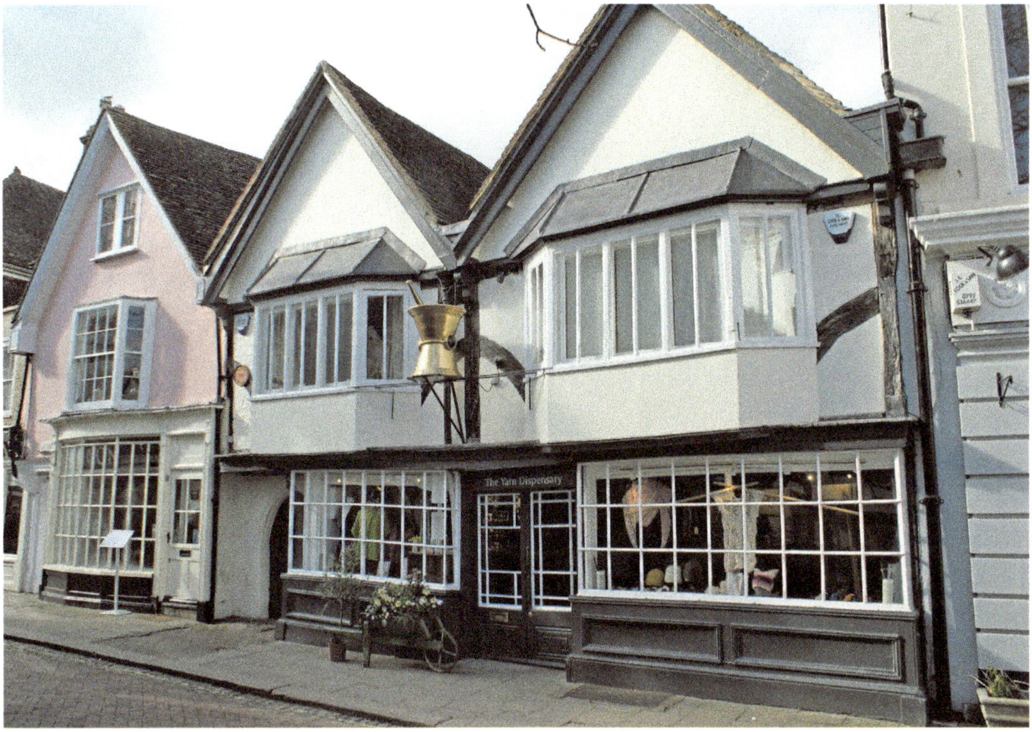

Yarn Dispensary.

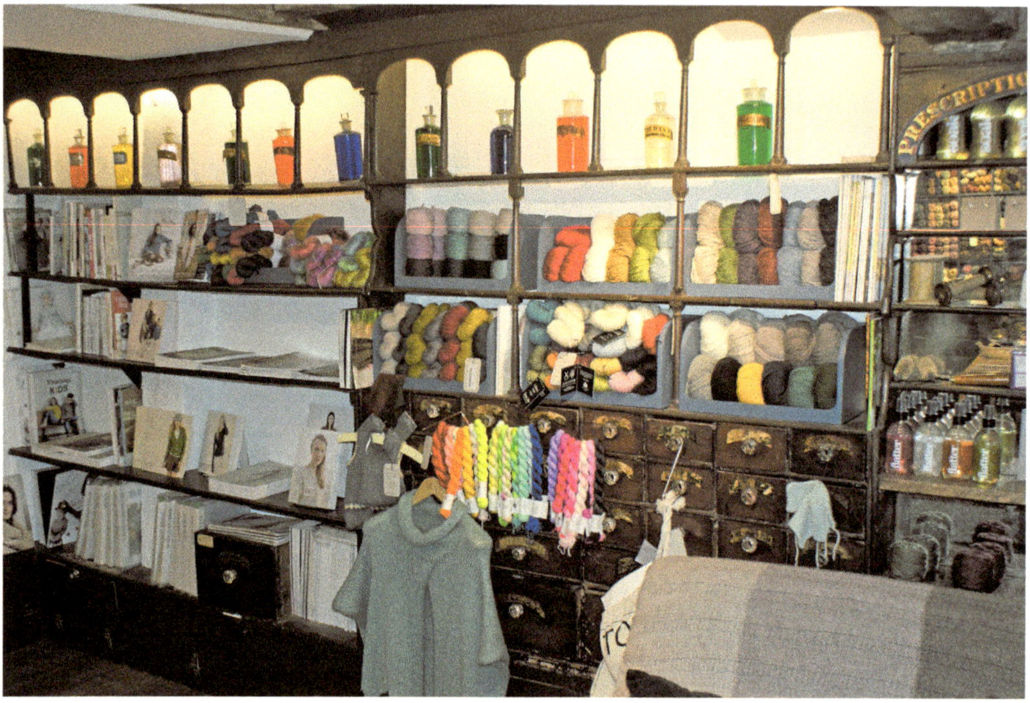

Wool stored in chemist shop fittings.

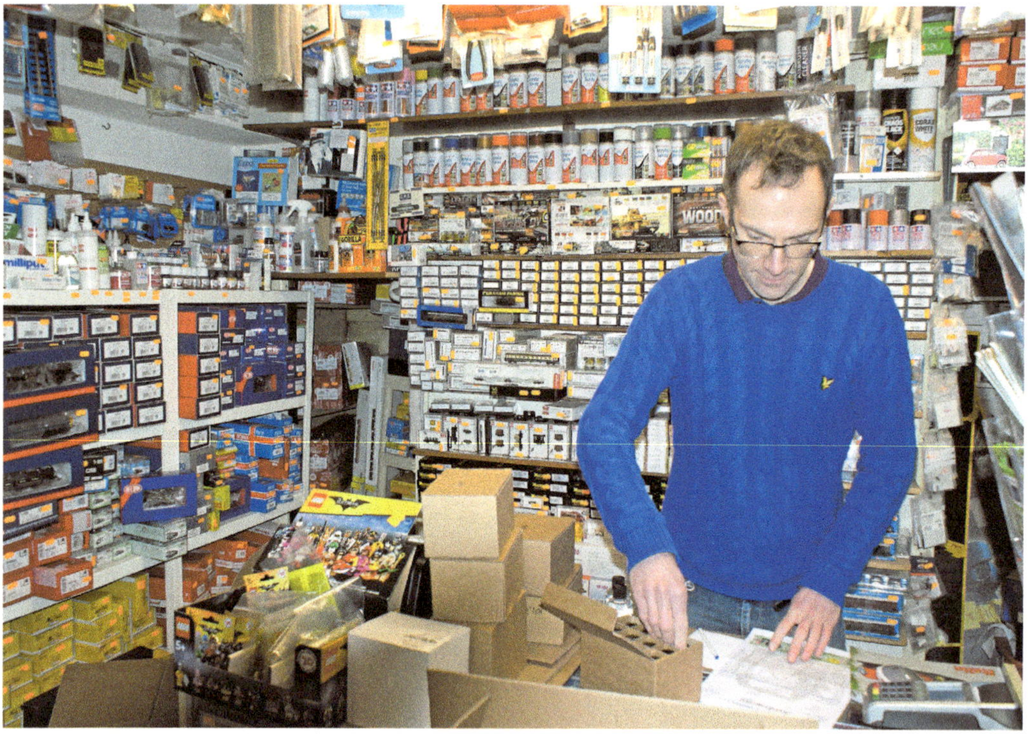

Harvey Alexander, who runs The Hobby Shop.

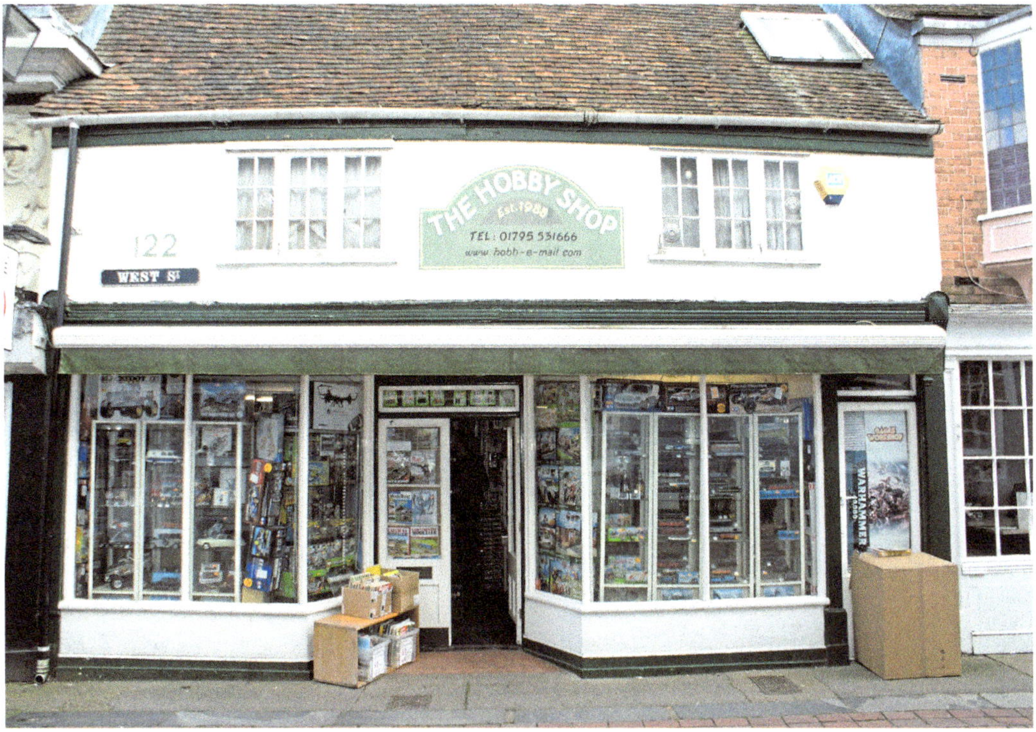

The Hobby Shop, West Street.

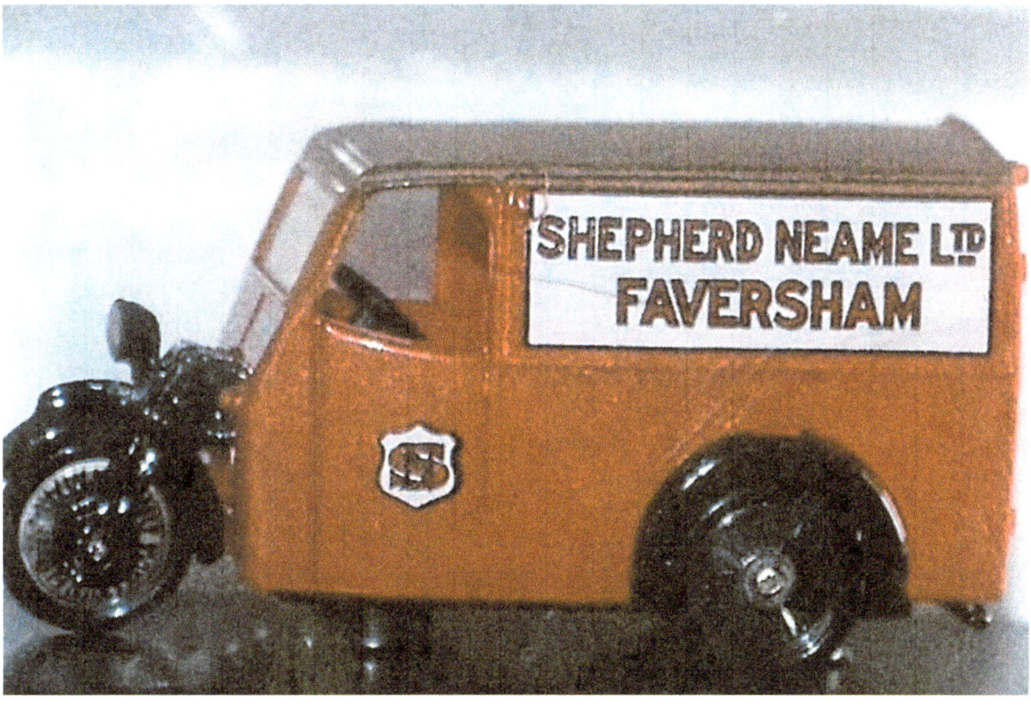

Model of 'Sheps' three-wheeled delivery van.

Turning right into West Street the flow of unusual shops continues. Soon one is drawn into the wonderful interior of Hobby Shop. Successfully run by Harvey Alexander for the past twenty-eight years, he stocks an exciting range of 00 gauge railways. The example here of a three-wheeled Shepherd Neame delivery vehicle is the type of model that might be bought here.

Sadly, apart from the ubiquitous WHSmith, fewer and fewer towns boast of a bookshop. Amazon has undoubtedly affected this trend. Gloriously though, Faversham boasts a number of booksellers. Surely it is an indicator of this place's elevated cultural standards. Past Sentence is a terrific example. Packed with groaning shelves, they have a strong section on military history. Happily snapped among her diverse range of volumes is Kate Roland, who has been here for around fifteen years.

Further downhill is the Hat Shop. Rachael Thapa-Chhtri has traded here for three years, enjoying the challenge of supplying both ladies and gentlemen with the headgear of their choice. To promote the wearing of hats this enterprising businesswomen started Faversham Hat Festival. Appropriately, this occurs on Easter Saturday and is in its fourth year.

Somewhat out of town is Macnade Fine Foods. It is the largest food hall in the South East and is run with a real passion by its proprietors and staff. Romantically the business began as a pick your own market garden managed by an Italian called Renato, who married a Kentish farmer's daughter named Patricia. No longer do they cultivate this land. However, their love of purveying top-quality and unusual foods has mushroomed into an organisation employing fifty staff. So extensive is the range of comestibles that some wags have given it the soubriquet Kent's Harrods's Food Hall! Lots of fruits and vegetables are sourced locally as there is a preference for these nearby supplies. Neighbouring meat producers are similarly prioritised.

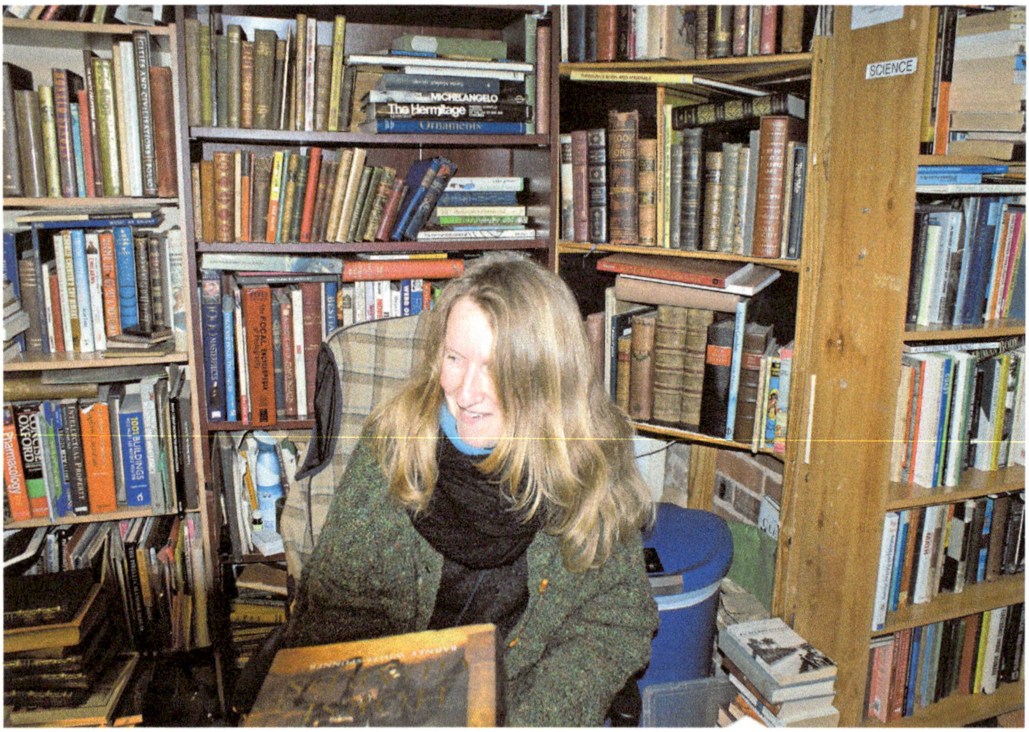

Kate Roland of bookshop Past Sentence.

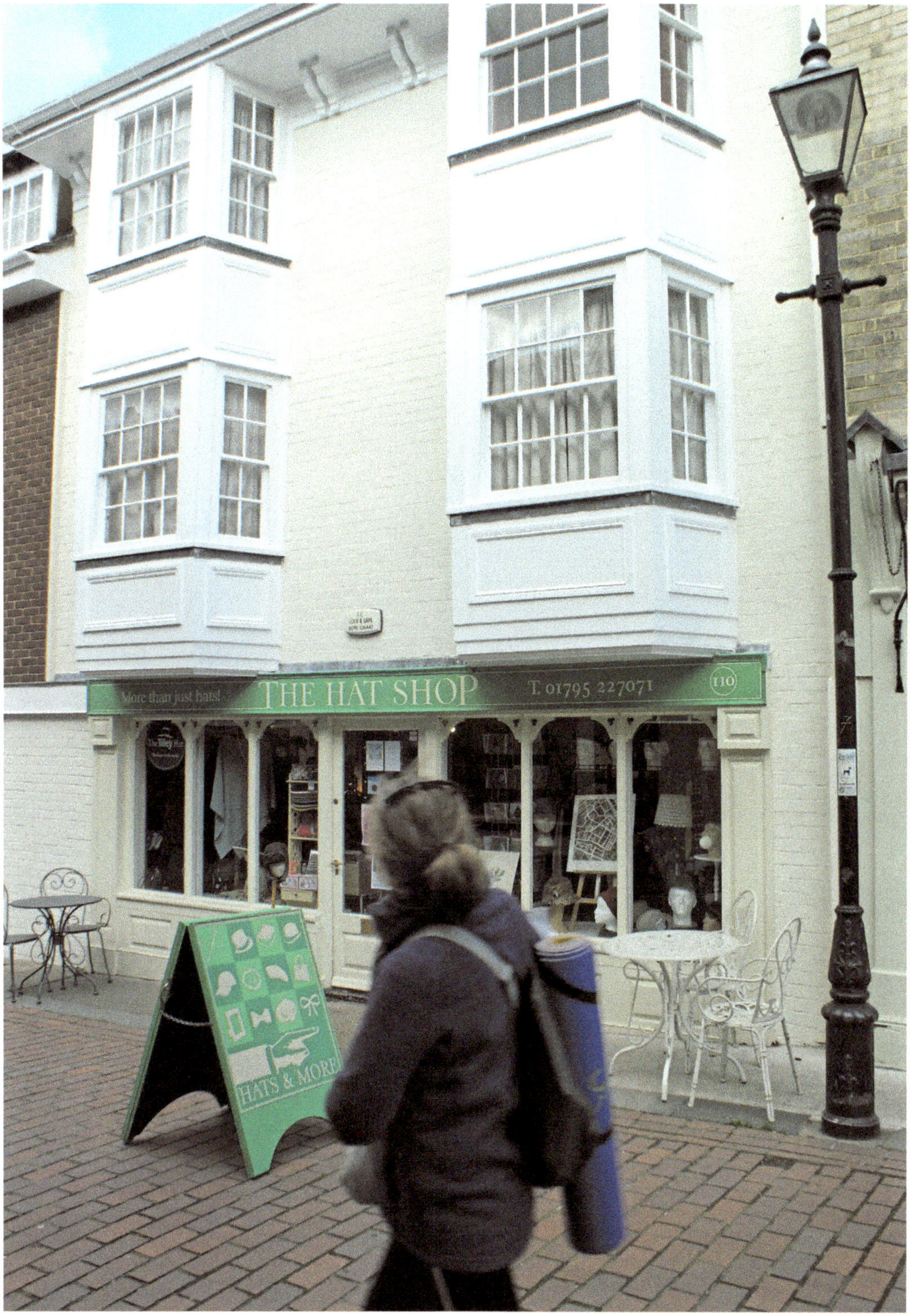

The Hat Shop, West Street.

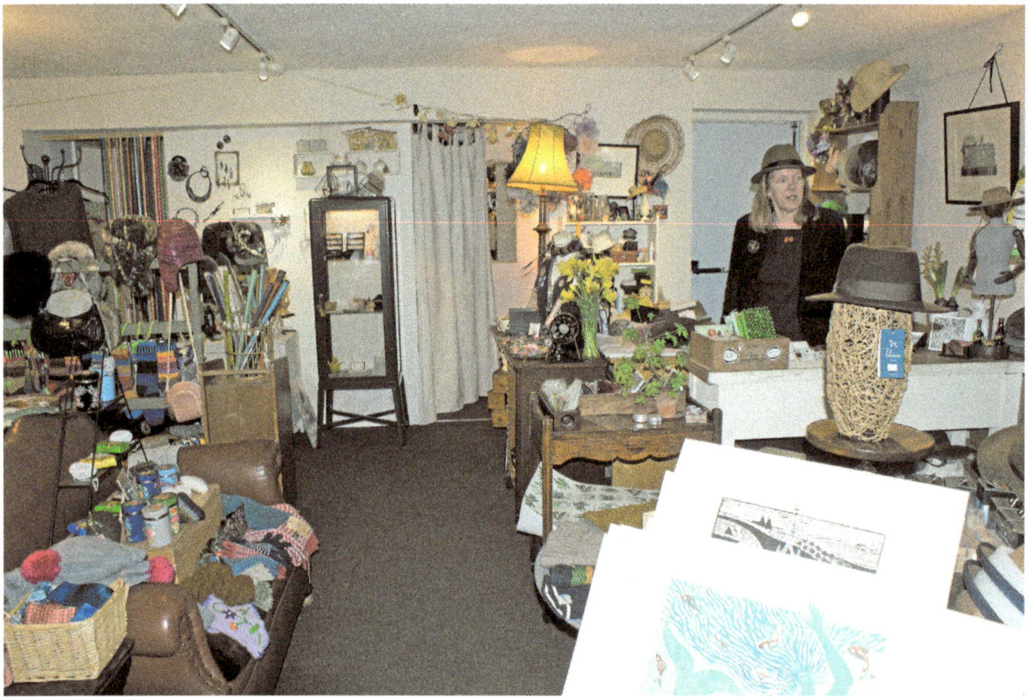

Rachael Thapa-Chhtri, who runs The Hat Shop.

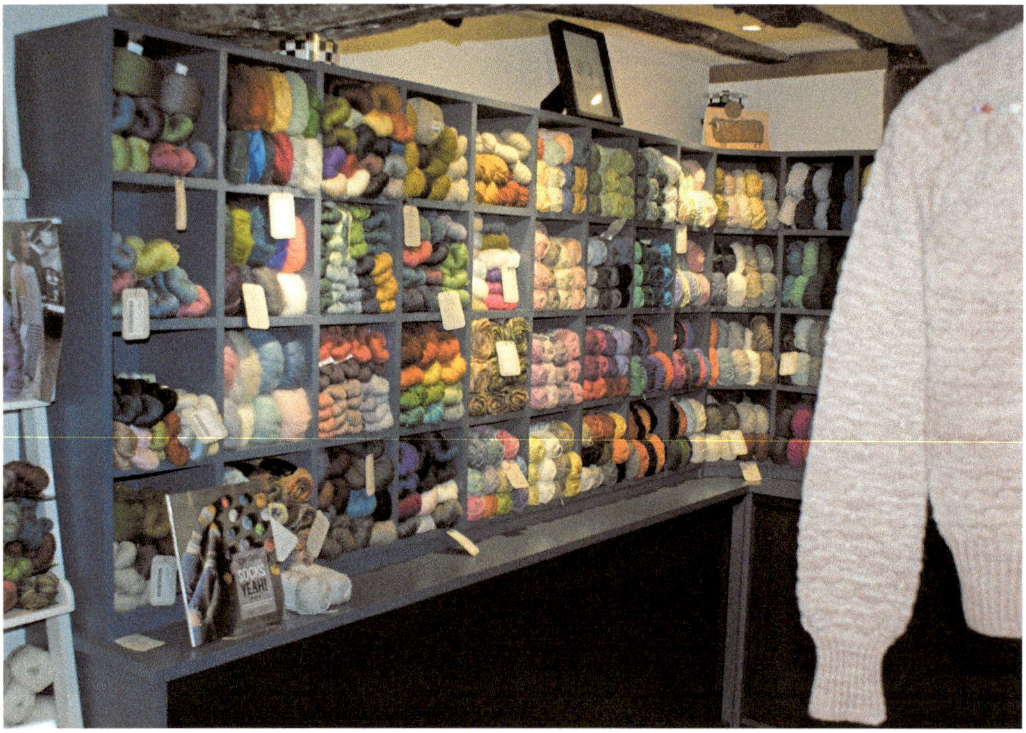

Extensive range of exclusive wools at Yarn Dispensary.

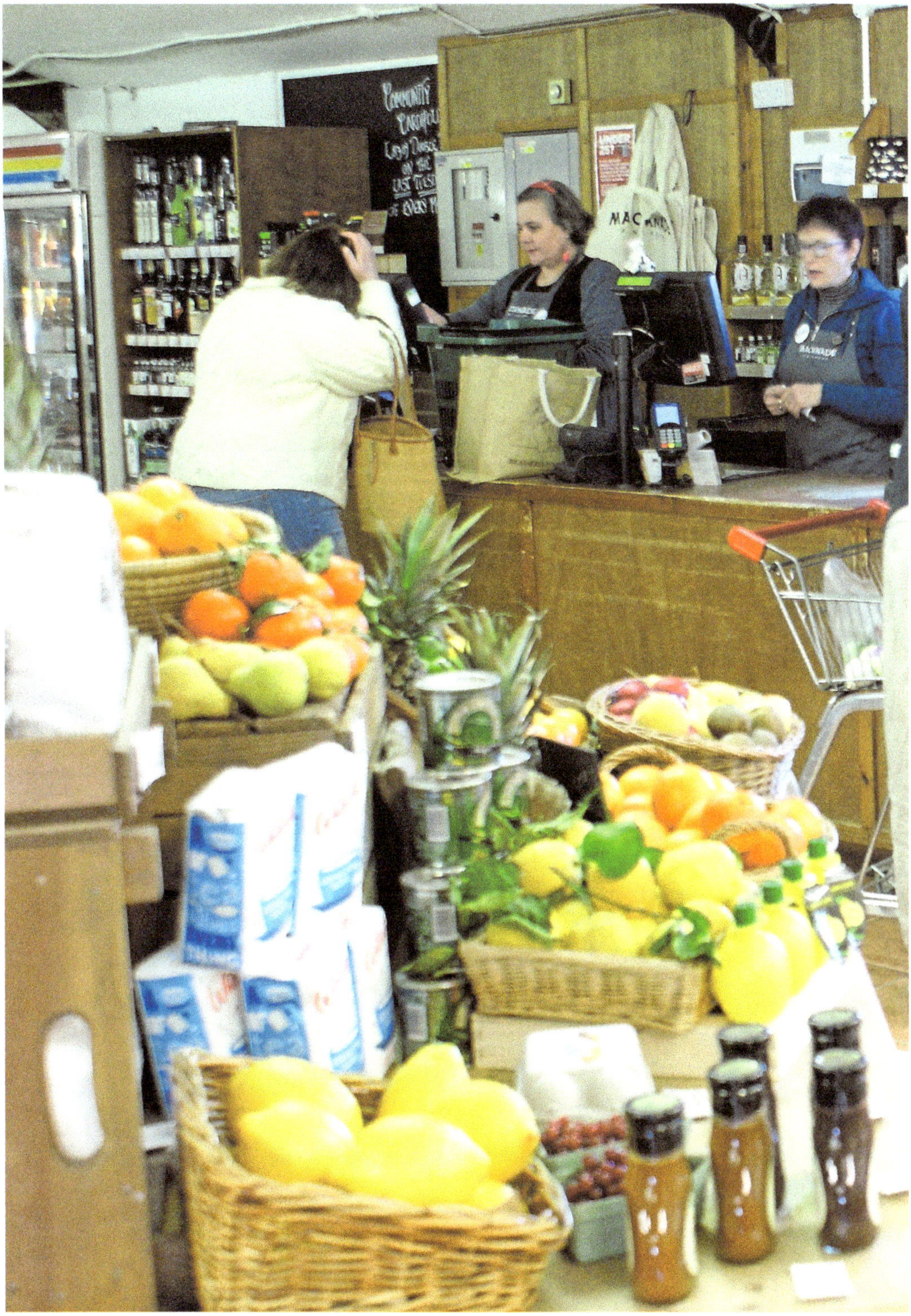

Checkout at Macnade Fine Foods.

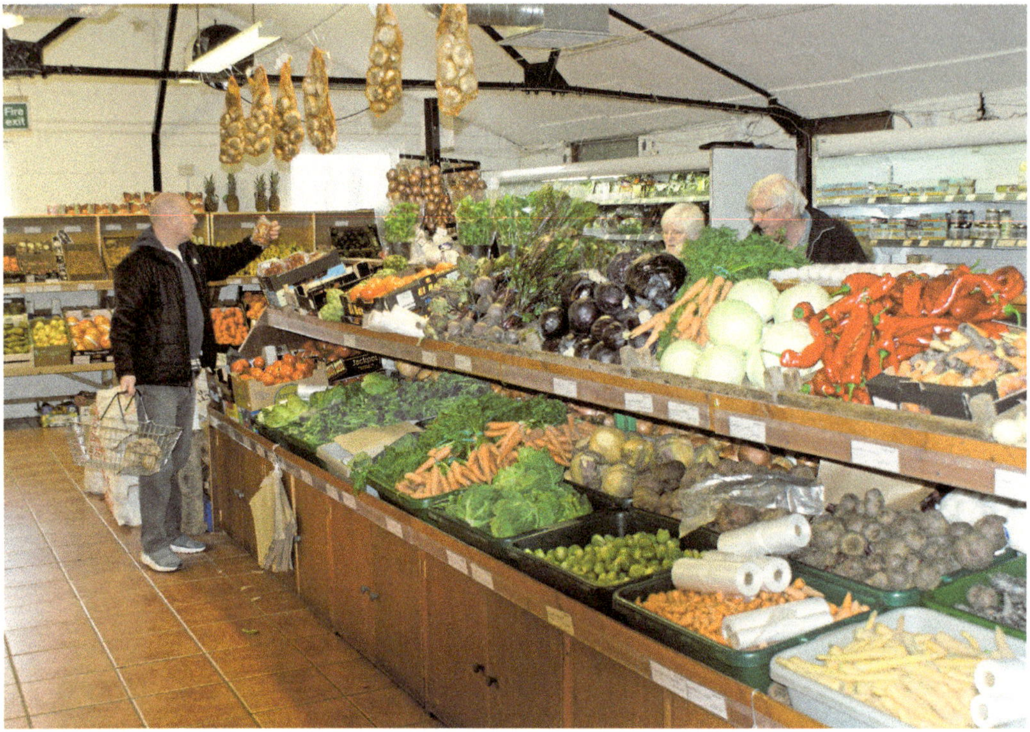

Perfectly fresh produce at Macnade Fine Foods.

The shop, inclusive of restaurant, is based in an incongruous structure built on part of a farm acquired in 1847 by ancestors of the owning family. Rightly this valuable asset to Faversham's reputation has received many awards. They have regularly won Taste of Kent retailer of the year and Kent Life Food and Drink prize. In turn their suppliers are often award winners too. For example they sell 'Shaggy's Beard' camembert, which was rated best goats cheese at the International Cheese awards.

Obviously, good butchers exist in this town, which is the focus for top livestock breeders. Barkaways and Colin Graham of Brogdale are two prime examples; the latter's counters of lean appetising cuts are displayed in the photograph overleaf.

Fine cuisine can be found at the prestigious Read's restaurant with rooms nearby. Here fine food is impeccably served with crisp white napery and an ambient air of experienced competence.

Too many other good eateries in pubs, restaurants and cafés exist for them all to be itemised individually. Another exception to this rule, however, is Judd's Folly Hotel. This sits atop a hill in stately parkland at the western side of town on the A2, or Watling Street. Once this beautiful location was the site of a Roman fortress and relics of their previous occupation have been excavated here, while a few hundred yards away there are the ruins of a pagan mausoleum. It is named after a seventeenth-century gunpowder and salvage mogul who was on the Parliamentarian side during the Civil War. With his wealth he built a seat here, but the freehold was confiscated after the Restoration, although he was permitted to stay on as a leaseholder. Hence its title Judd's Folly. A devastating fire destroyed most of the mansion in 1963. After reconstruction only the old kitchen remained. This has been converted into an attractive bar with the old spit in place over the fireplace as a reminder of past times. Garry Underwood, the bar manager, is shown later serving drinks.

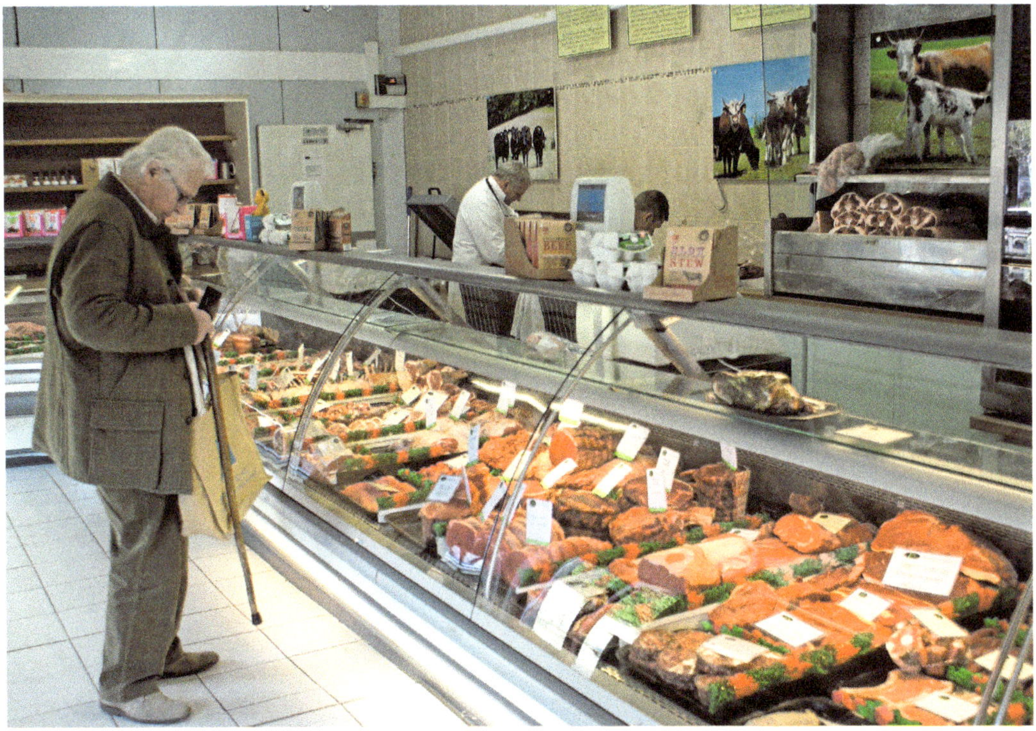

Top-quality butchery – Macnade.

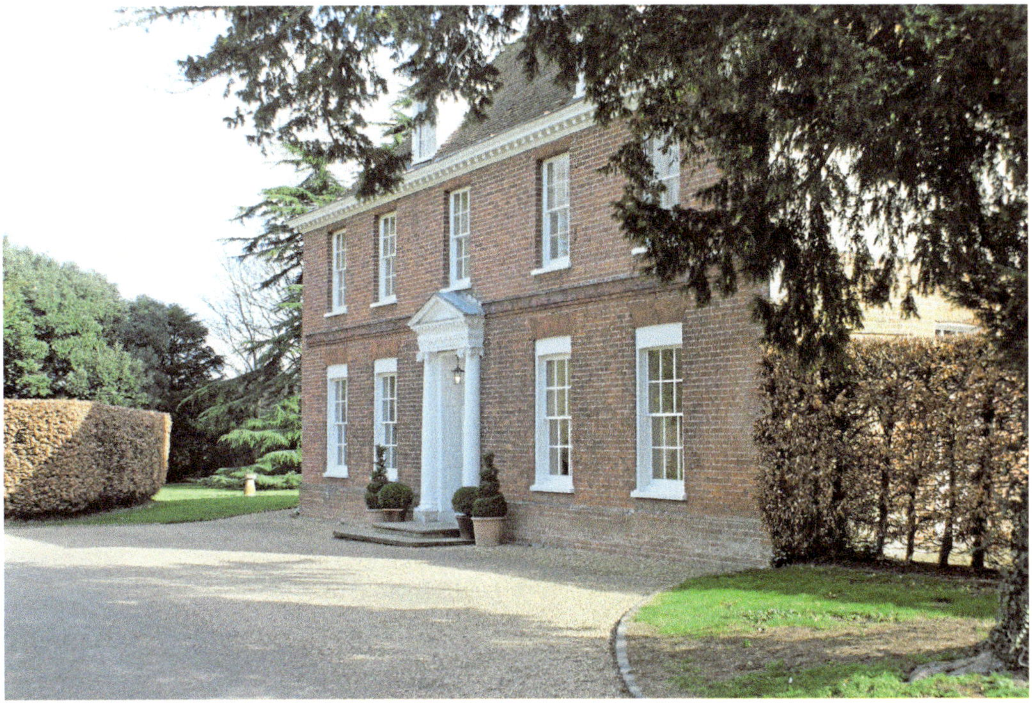

Read's restaurant with rooms.

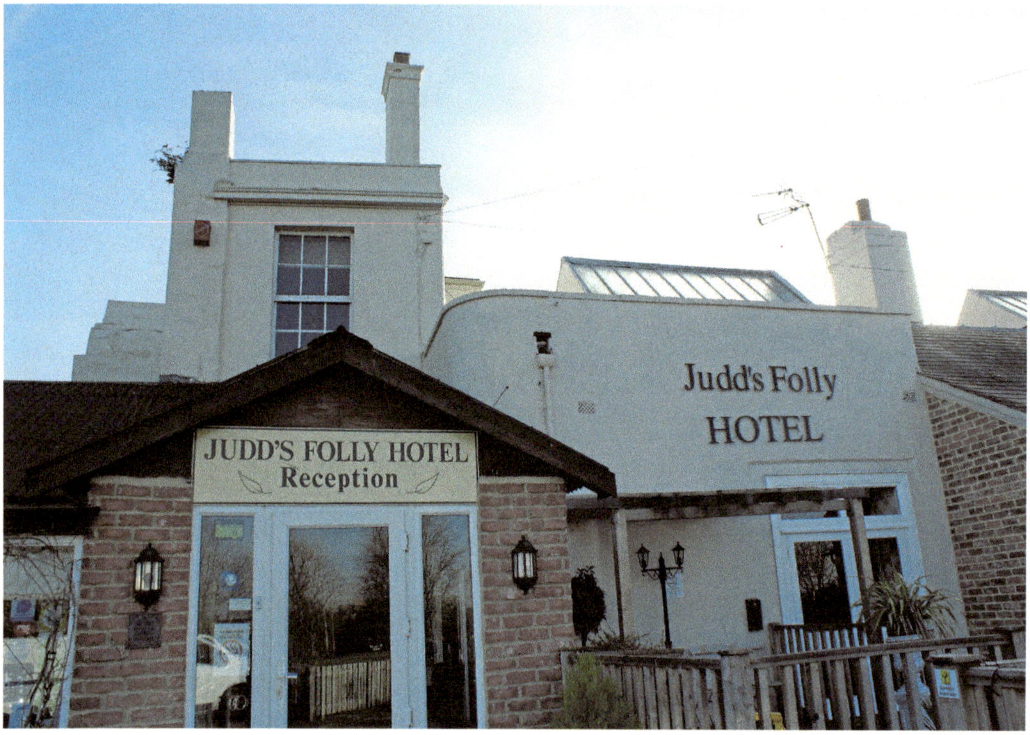

Judd's Folly Hotel.

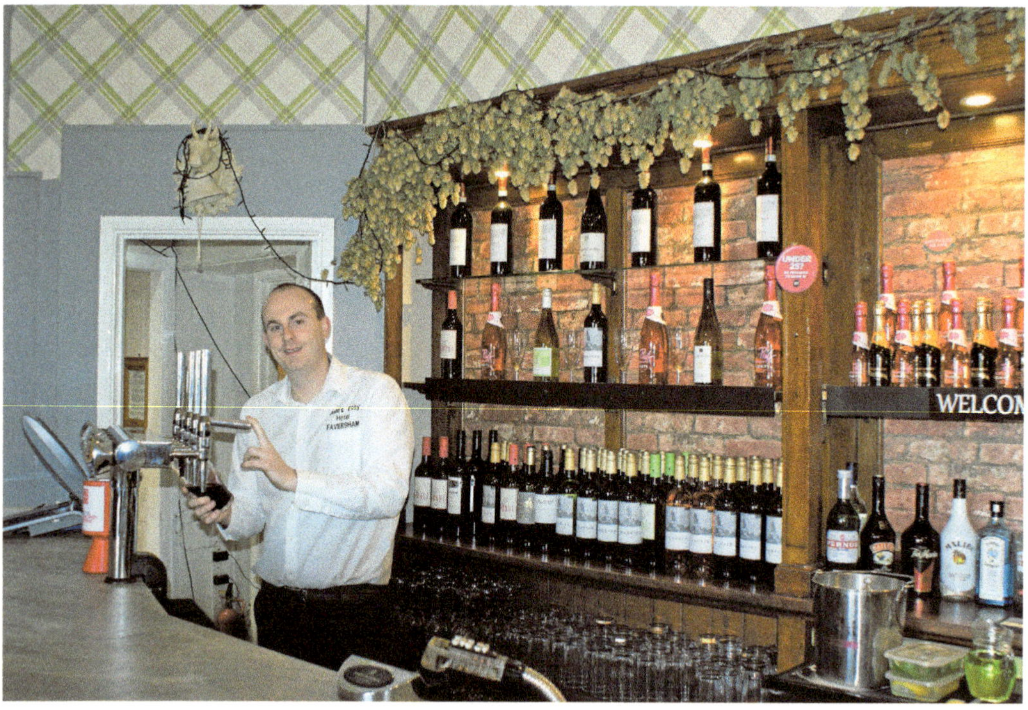

Gary Underwood, bar manager at Judd's Folly Hotel.

MISCELLANY

BMM WESTON GROUP

No narrative about Faversham at work would be complete without mention of BMM Weston Group. This is a leading name in the design and manufacture of equipment used in medical and healthcare spheres. They are also involved in laundry presses and foundry sector products.

While serving a potentially huge market for sterilizers in hospitals and dentists, they obviously have to be made to a very high standard. High specification is also required for laboratory and pharmaceutical applications. Steam generators are another major product line. Constructed from stainless steel they are either electrically or steam-heated devices.

For many years this firm has made laundry machinery. Their ironing presses are sold worldwide where they can be found functioning for extensive years in hotels, prisons and dry cleaners.

Another very durable item made by BMM Weston are their green sand moulding machines. They are used in metal foundries and use the tried-and-trusted jolt/squeeze functionality.

Taking pride in being a manufacturer, everything this company produces is designed and made at their premises near Davington, Faversham. They use state-of-the-art machinery and fabricating processes. In this way equipment is engineered that can be trusted and relied on. Leading computer technology is employed for design and production. Additionally, all electrical and software for sale is designed in-house.

Relying on three core fundamentals – quality, strength and knowledge – their aim is to be at the forefront of its chosen fields of operation. Training is therefore a vital element of such success. Accordingly they have forged strong links with local schools, colleges and universities providing long-term apprentice and graduate intake. Overall this well-established business is proud to be part of this community where it employs many of the town's inhabitants.

THE ROYAL CINEMA

The Royal Cinema in Market Place started life as the Odeon in 1936. It was designed by Andrew Mather, who aimed to harmonise its appearance with its predominately historic surroundings. There are around 500 listed buildings in Faversham and one of the finest medieval streets in England. Tudorbethan cinemas were in any case highly fashionable during the interwar years. This example is one of only two left in the UK. Furthermore, there are currently less than 100 of the old-style large-screen picture houses remaining.

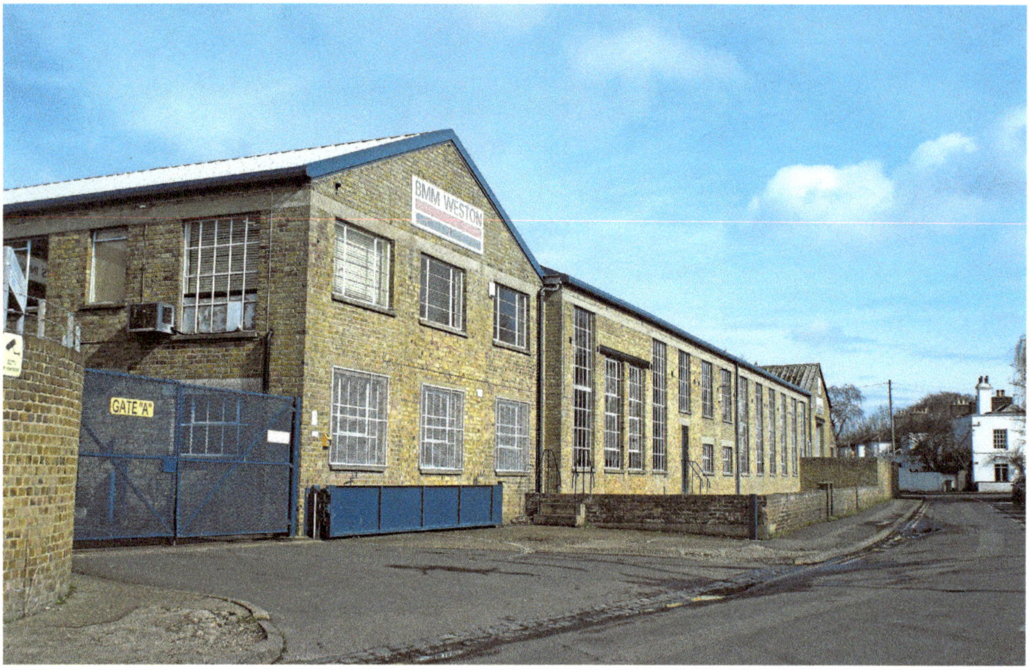

BMM Western Group works buildings.

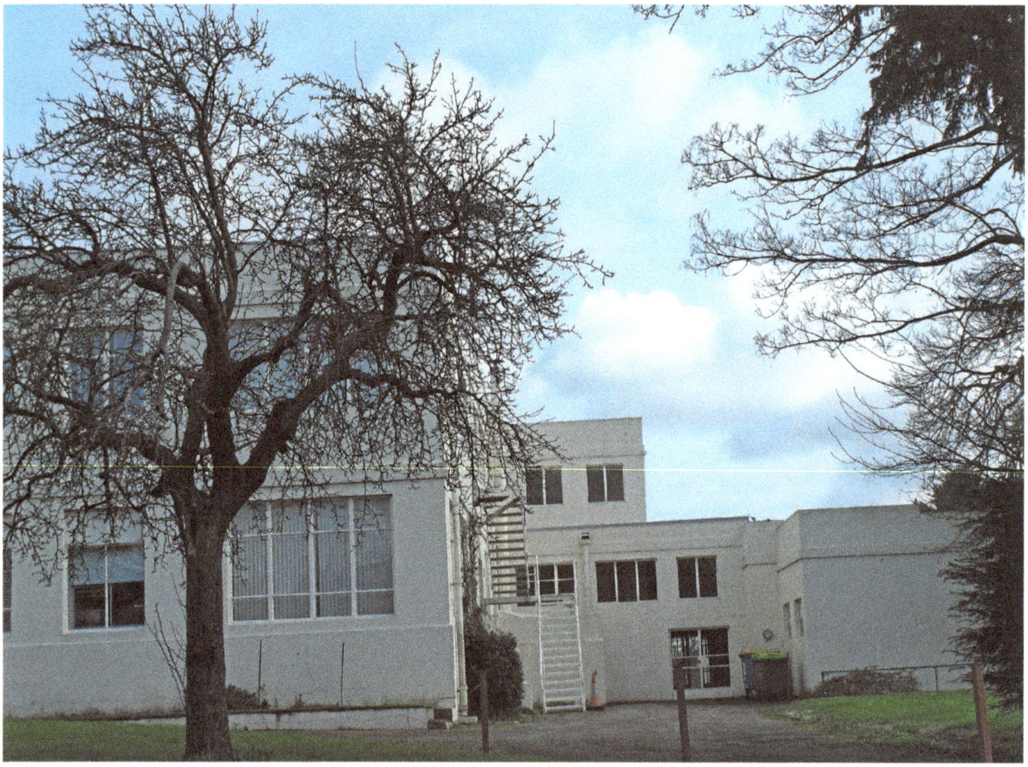

BMM Western Group offices.

Popularity of television impacted on audiences. Nonetheless, fortunately in 1994 Peter Baldock and Michael Harlow had foresight enough to reopen the Odeon/Classic and rename it.

Given this new lease of life, a bright future followed with judicial repairs, improvements and sensible choice of films. Feature films, and productions for children, suit popular tastes. More serious subjects are often selected for Faversham Film Society. By catering for everyone a successful formulae has been devised.

Other important minor details are paid attention to and appreciated by loyal regular patrons. Staff are uniformed, polite and helpful. Happily the tariff of £5 per head is reasonable and not subject to frequent irritating increases. Best of all the large, red, plush-seated auditorium, which once seated 700, is comfortable and nostalgically redolent of an age when going to the 'flicks' was a thrilling experience. Held in much affection by townsfolk, this gem is fortunately a Grade II-listed building.

Outside there can be found a plaque provided by the British Film Institution celebrating a Century of Cinema in 1996. This coincided with the Royal's 60th Anniversary. Another similar commemorative plaque can be found at No. 74 West Street – once the home of Hollywood pioneer Albert E. Smith (co-founder of Vitagraph Studios and winner of a special Oscar in 1947).

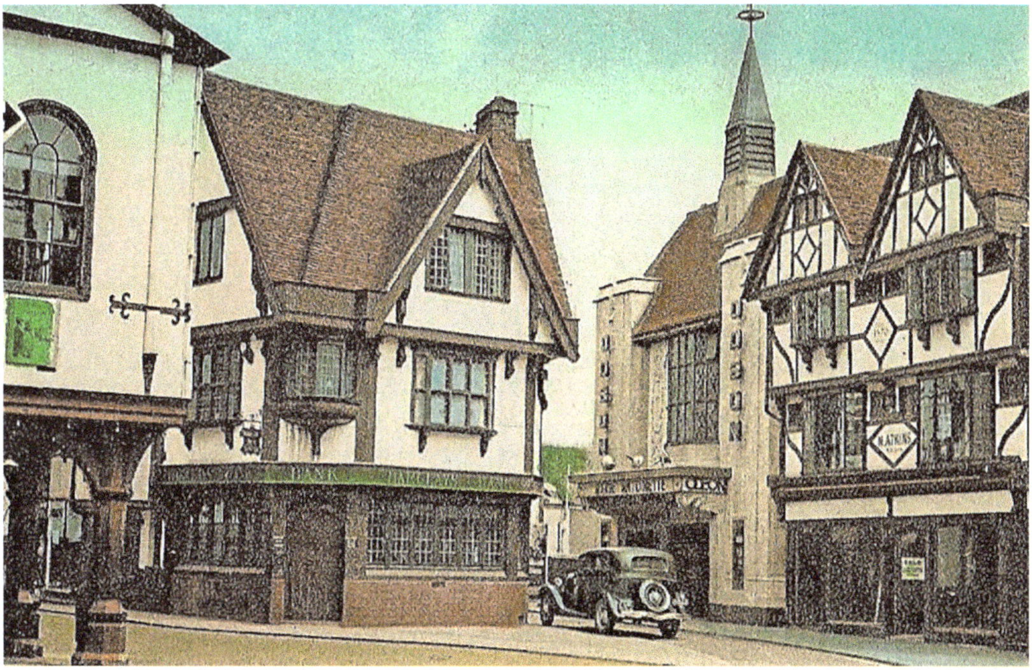

Odeon Cinema, c. 1930s.

FAVERSHAM SWIMMING BATHS

Faversham Swimming Baths were built in two phases. The first (1964) was an outdoor pool of 33 metres with three diving boards of 1 m, 2 m and 3 m. Then in 1993 an indoor pool of 25 metres was opened by champion swimmer Nick Gillingham MBE. This complex also has a learner pool with Jacuzzi and beach area. Outside, a toddlers' pool and fun rapids ride is conveniently placed next to a grassed picnic spot, but outdoor facilities are only open during summer months.

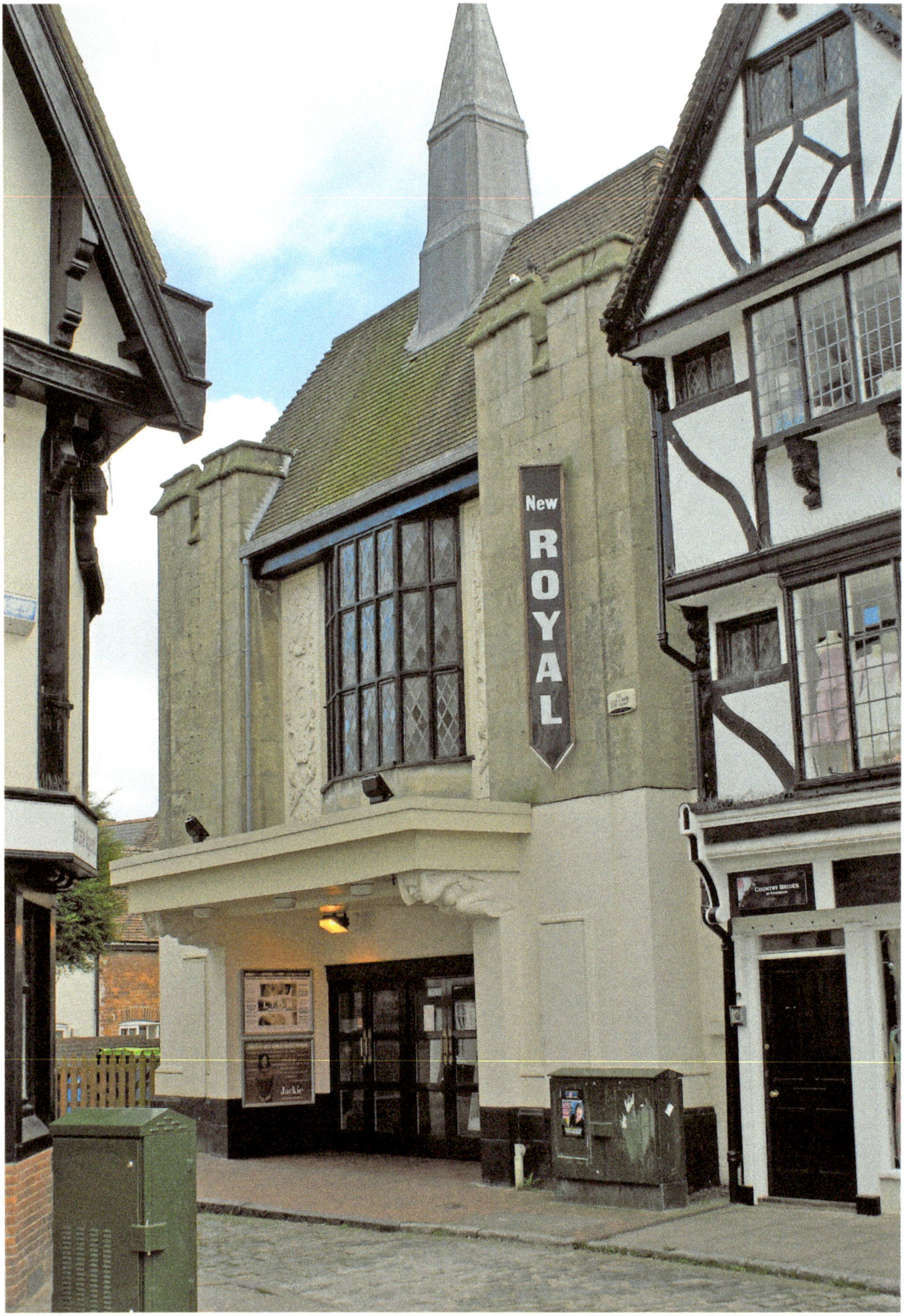

Royal Cinema today.

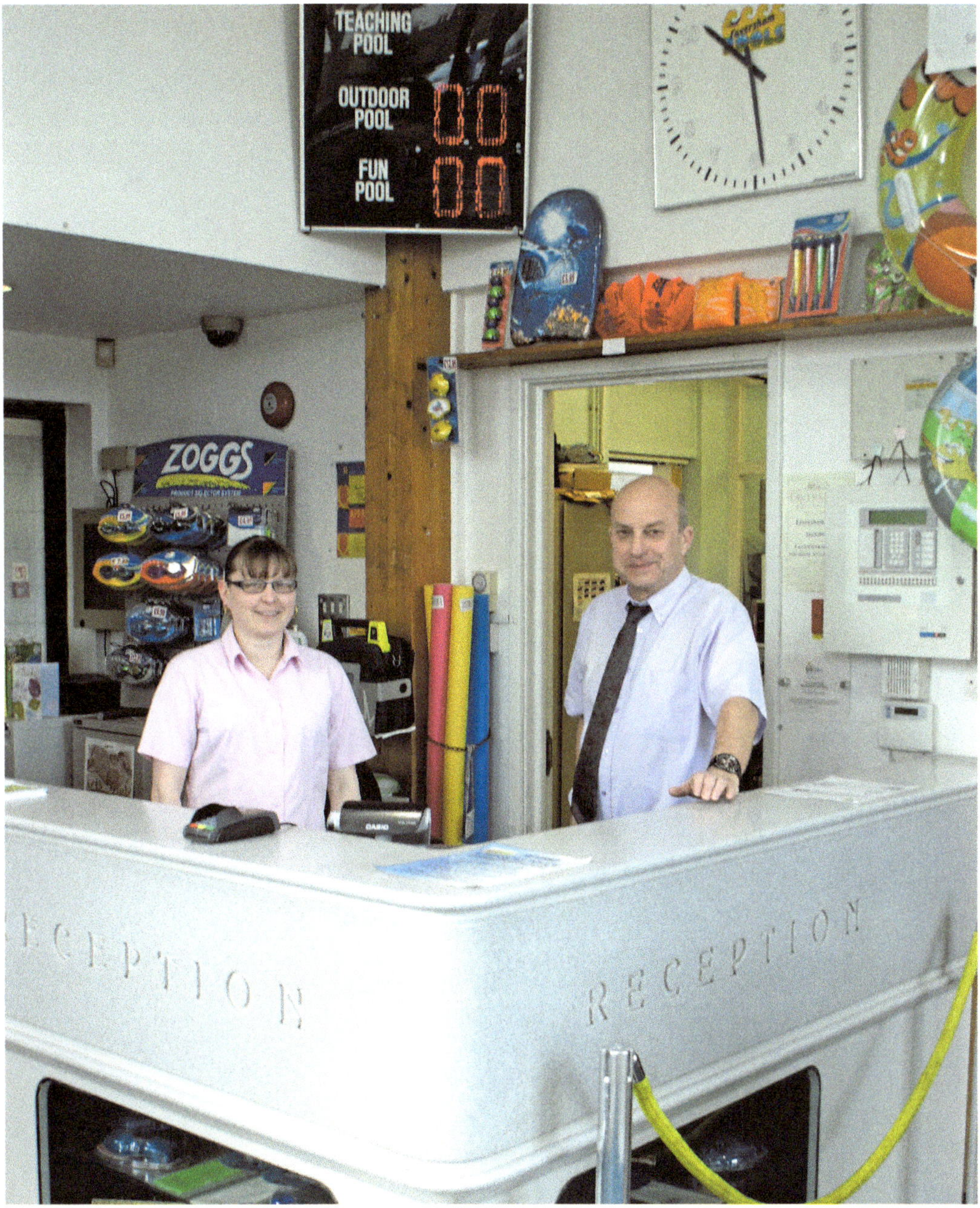

Mikaela Drake and Roger Lake eager to greet swimmers at Faversham Baths.

Two clubs enjoy this efficiently run amenity. Faversham Swimming Club has over 300 members with ages ranging from five to eighty-five. Water polo and synchronised swimming is practised up to national standards. Swale Tri Club arrange coaching sessions for technique improvement.

Lido staff, who include Roger Lake and Mikaela Drake (seen above behind the reception desk) are happy to assist the public with bookings for lessons, etc. Astonishingly some intrepid swimmers even turn up for their regular dip on certain days as early as 6 a.m.

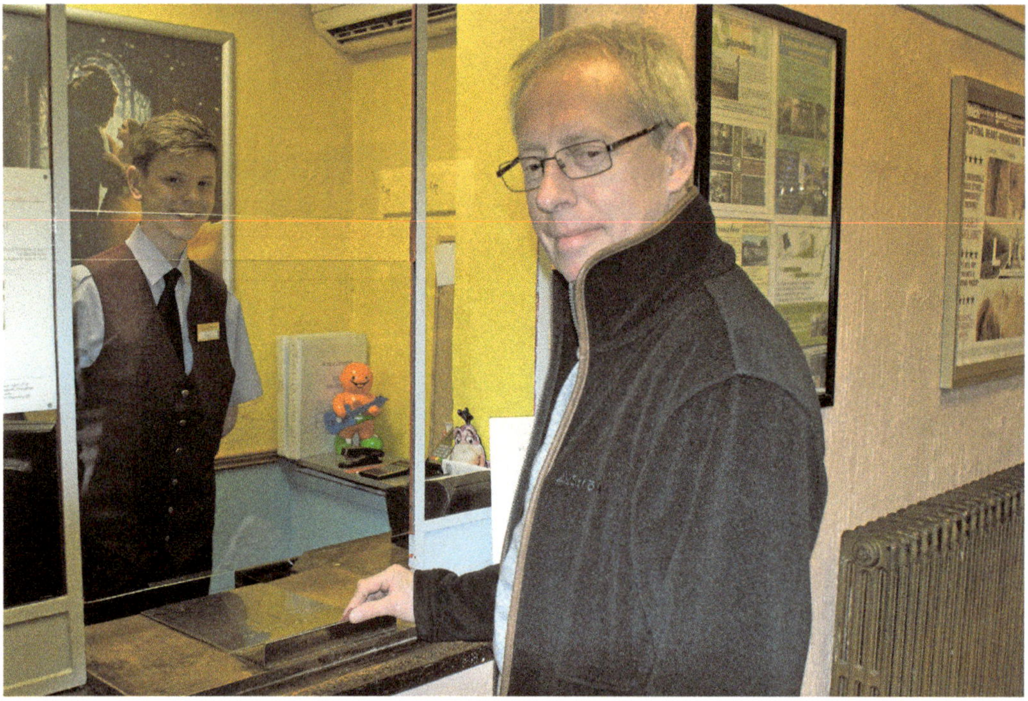

Mr Hollis, a regular film fan, at a kiosk manned by a smartly uniformed attendant.

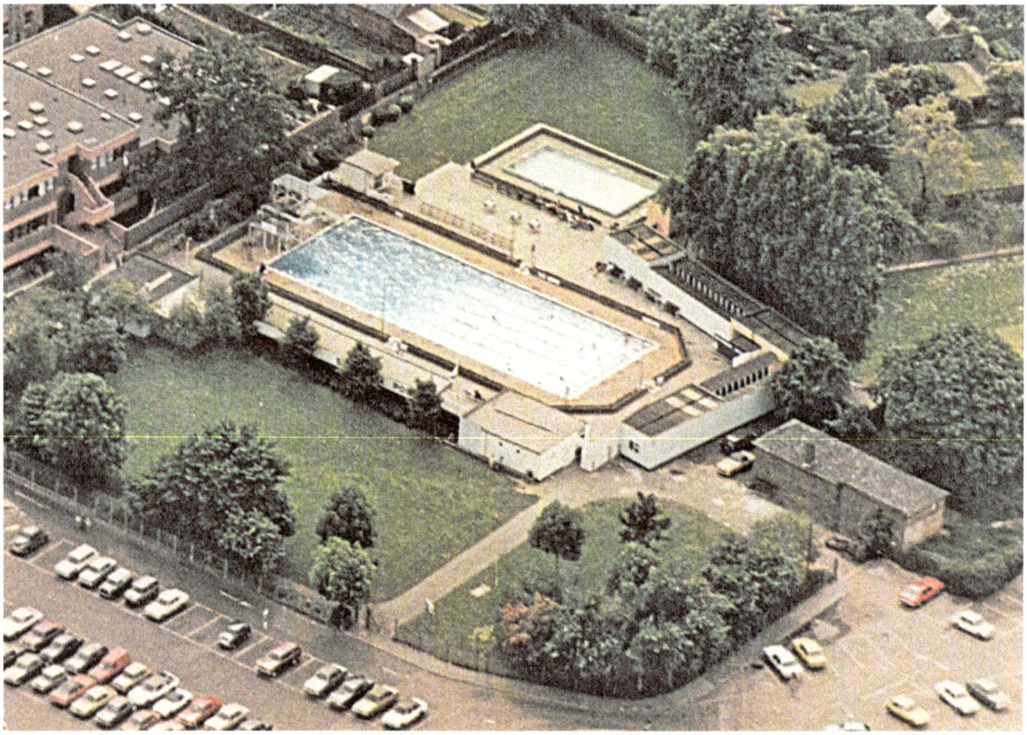

Open-air baths before addition of adjacent enclosed pool.

DOCTORS

Faversham doctors of a bygone age can be seen on this page posing for a group portrait by a plate glass camera. They look to be confident and full of self-esteem with canvas stretchers lying at their feet.

Today the town has been blessed by Newton Place Surgery in particular. Its purpose-built headquarters house staff caring for some 17,000 patients. They are rated among the top two surgeries in Swale District and top five in the Canterbury and Faversham District for patient satisfaction. Doctors and nurses take pride in offering the highest standard of medical care. Conveniently, early and late appointments are available as well as normal daytime ones.

SCHOOLS

There are two good secondary schools preparing the children of Faversham for work or further education. Serving these are fine infant and primary ones. Less mindless disciplinary strictness that is implicit in the regimental stiffness shown in a later sepia photograh has evolved, but both senior schools expect good behaviour. Queen Elizabeth's Grammar School is a forward-thinking co-educational selective school set in the heart of town with over 1,000 pupils. Whereas, Abbey School is a mixed secondary school of a similar size located south of the main A2 road. Its playing fields are pictured on page 75 with a sign quoting a commendation from Ofsted reporters.

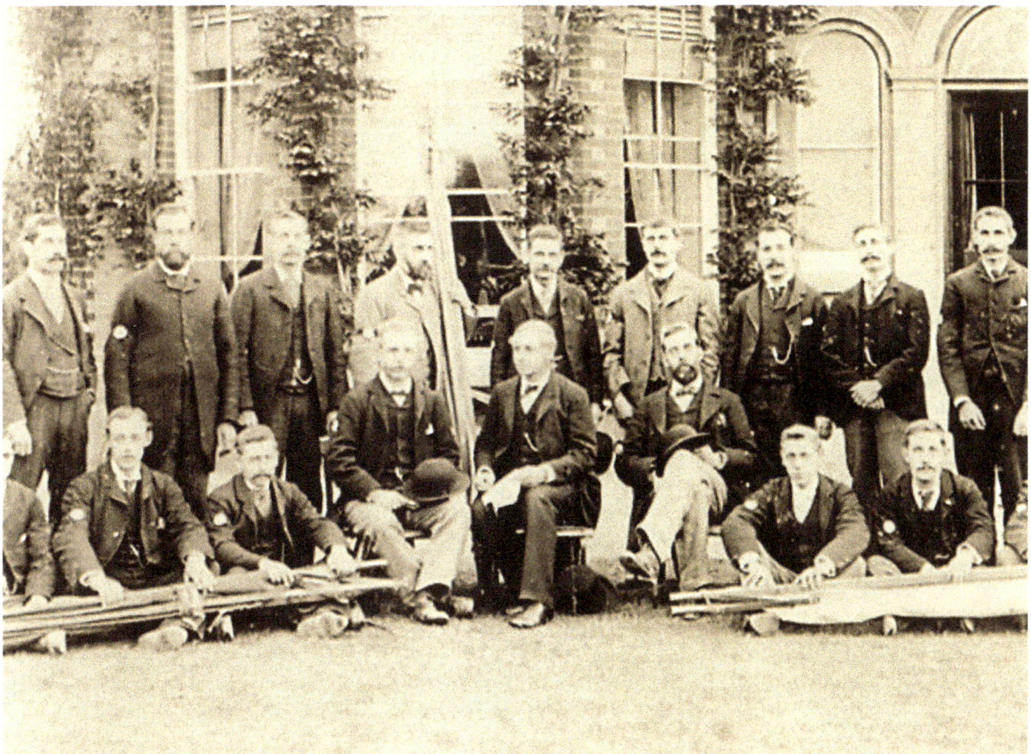

Rare portrait of Faversham's erstwhile doctors.

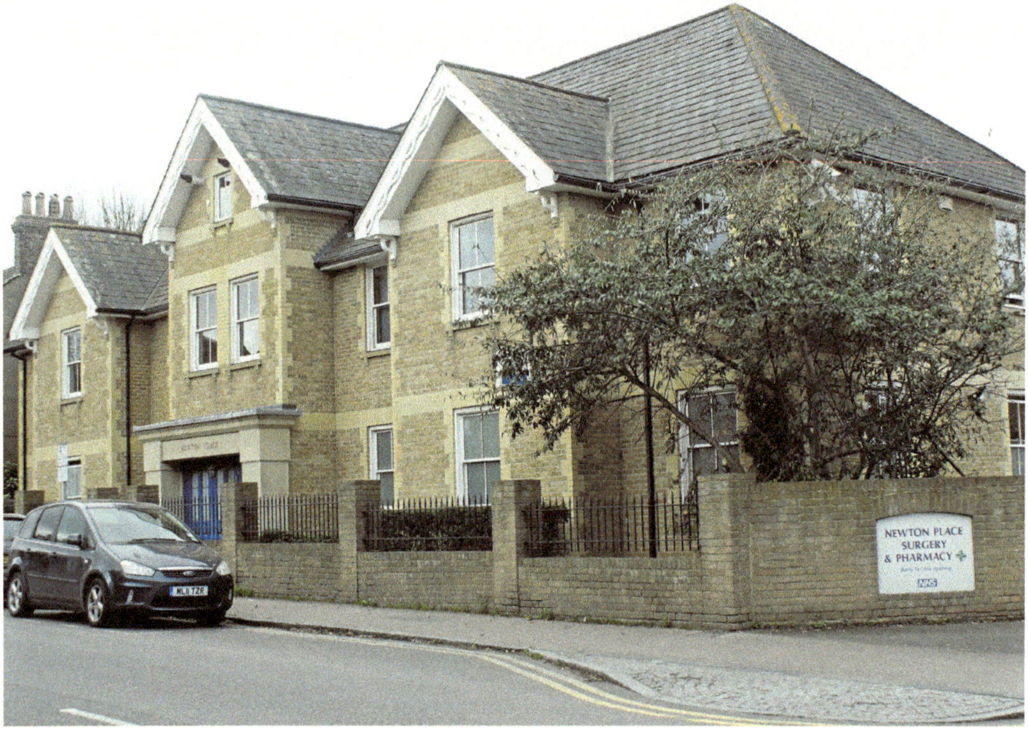

Newton Place Surgery.

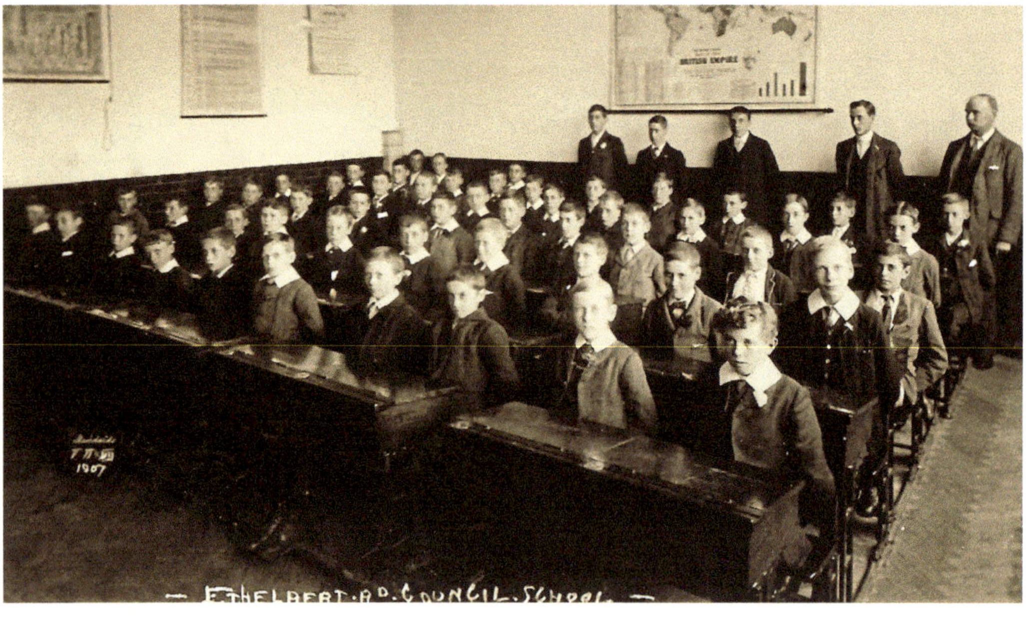

Strict discipline within a schoolroom of yesteryear.

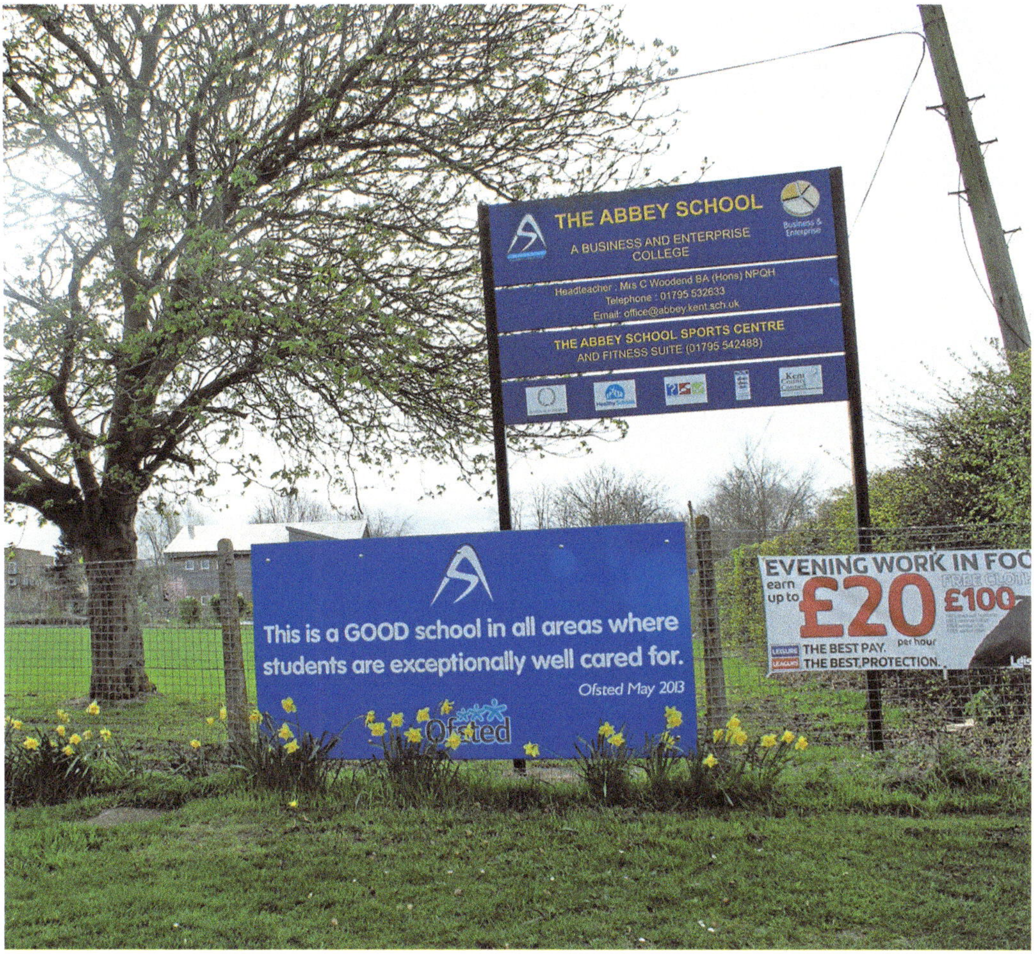

Rolling school playing fields parallel to Watling Street.

RAILWAY

The railway came to Faversham in 1858 when the East Kent Railway built its first station here. An improved replacement came with London, Chatham and Dover taking over in the last years of the nineteenth century. This solid Grade II-listed structure is well maintained by current operators Southeastern. The plethora of cast-iron rafters and railings are resplendent in thick coats of shinny paint.

Different platforms are allocated for four main tracks as this is where the line divides with one going north-east to Ramsgate via Hernbay and the other to Dover via Canterbury. An old spur line to Standard Quay has long been abandoned through disuse. Electrification of the line came in 1959 so that steam locomotives (like the one seen at the top of page 76 pulling away), were broken up for scrap. Although dirty and requiring strenuous sweaty work, they were reliable and not much slower than trains of nowadays. The present journey time to Victoria is seventy minutes. However, in 2009, a high-speed service was introduced to St Pancras with a typical journey time of sixty-five minutes.

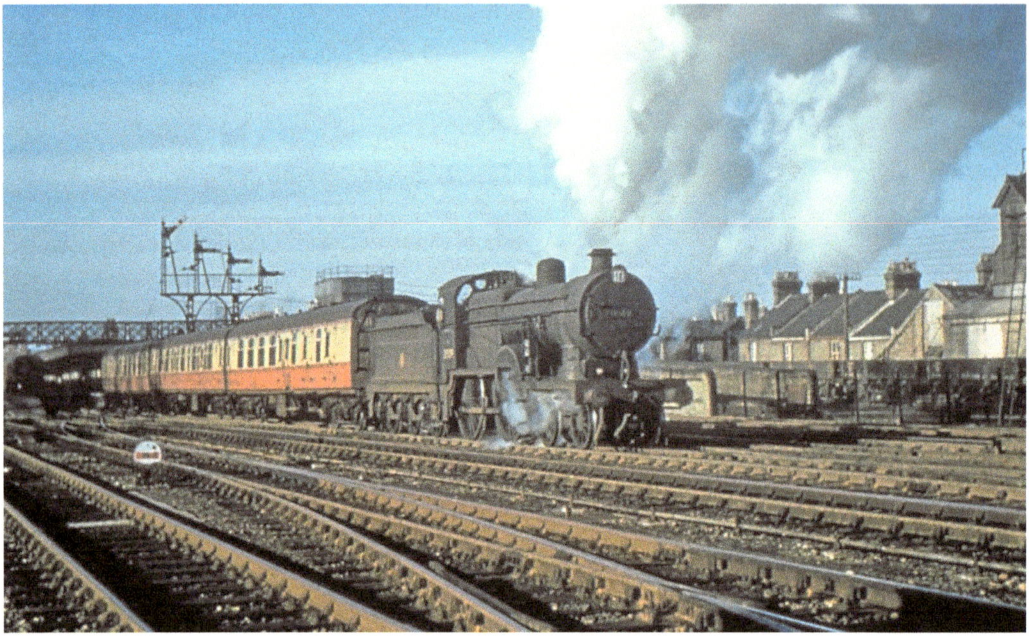

The age of steam at Faversham railway station.

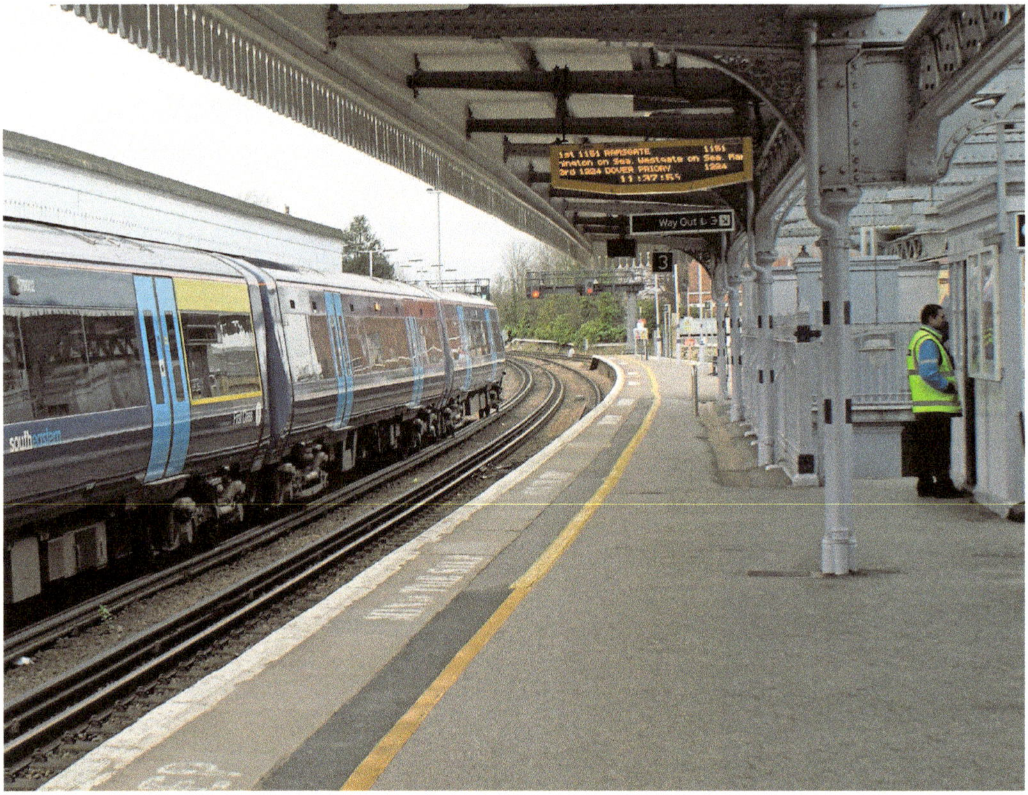

Less polluting rolling stock on its passage past platforms.

ART AND WORKSHOPS

Creek Creative Studios in Abbey Street is a collection of workshops, studios and galleries where some forty-five artists and artisans learn and work. It is based in an extensive former Victorian brewery, but still close enough to the centre of town to attract customers to its shop and café. The former offers a delightful range of locally crafted affordable wares. While the latter offers delicious light lunches and fabulous cakes using fine seasonal and closely sourced ingredients. Thoughtfully, they offer many 'free from' options.

Workshops provide permanent bases for artisans to work and also run training courses for the general public. Galleries are available on a temporary basis for artists to display their latest creations. Co-director Anne Mclaren says 'they are a friendly, flexible not-for profit organisation'. A good example of activity here is Alex Law's School of Upholstery. He is photographed on the next page assisting students in the use and application of materials for their projects.

In a peaceful cellar Justin Wood can be seen proudly surrounded by an exhibition of his unique assembly of silver crafted insects mounted on wooden backgrounds. He says that his work is a culmination of his life's experiences and passions. Learning the basic techniques of casting silver while training to be a dental technician, he went on to have a career in pest control. This gave him an insight into the world of insects and their kind. Combined with a lifetime love of collecting naturally sculptured wood, these three aspects are amalgamated to produce strikingly original physical results. A wonderfully literarily or philosophically poetic extra dimension is added by carefully considered titles for these creations.

WAREHOUSE AND RESTORATION

The Bike Warehouse in Preston Street stocks an impressive range of cycles and equipment. It is one of four such branches based in Kent. A considerable part of its business is concerned with servicing. Caught by the camera, at work, on page 80 is Keith Totten making adjustments to a customer's machine.

In researching potential subjects for this book I called upon South Eastern Coachworks in Preston Street. The warm and helpful reception I received from founder Chris Bichard soon made me realise that their motto 'Craftsmanship and Reliability' is no idle statement.

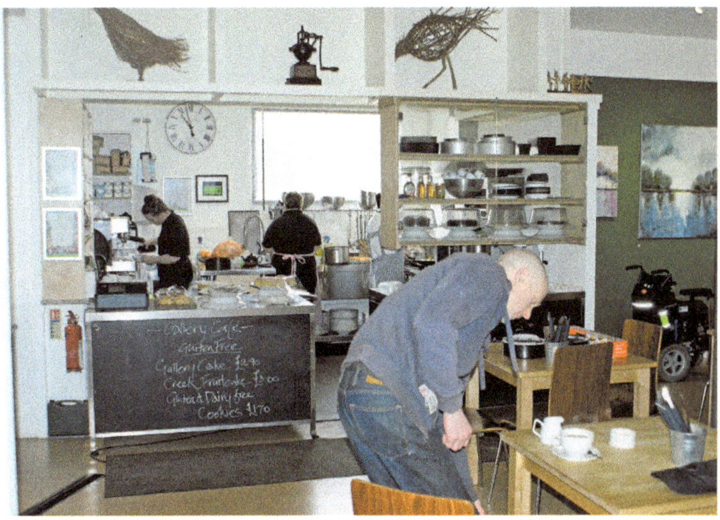

Café at Creek Creative Studios.

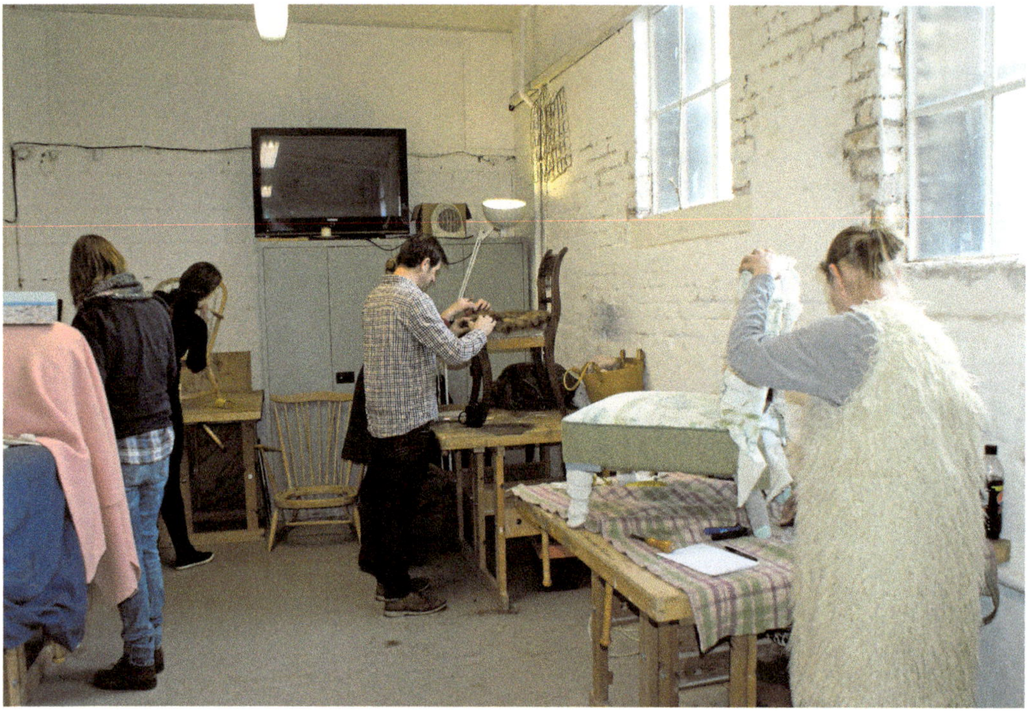

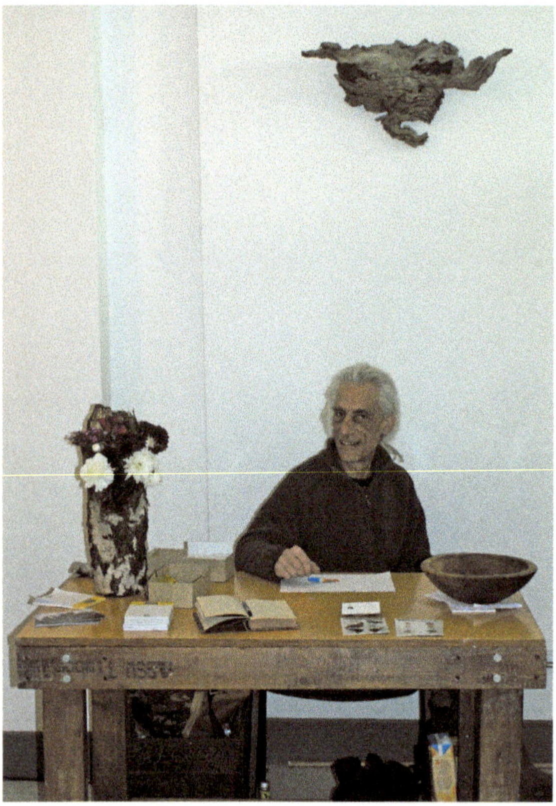

Above: Upholstery classes.

Left: Justin Wood, a uniquely talented artist.

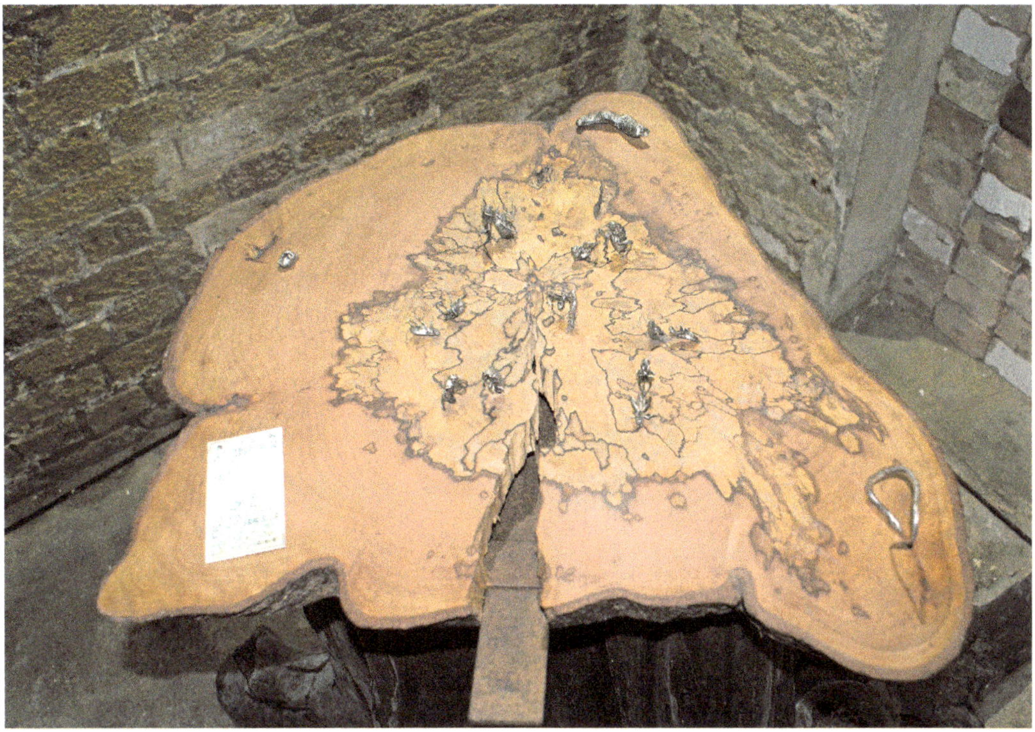

Exquisitely formed silver insects upon a wooden mount.

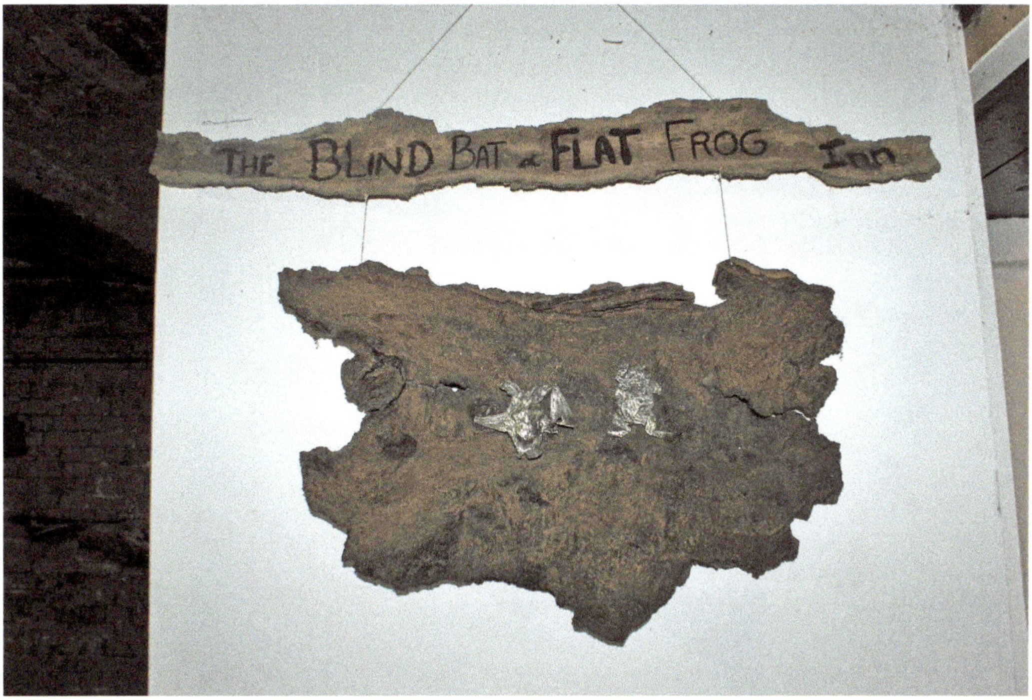

Work entitled *Blind Bat and Flat Frog Inn.*

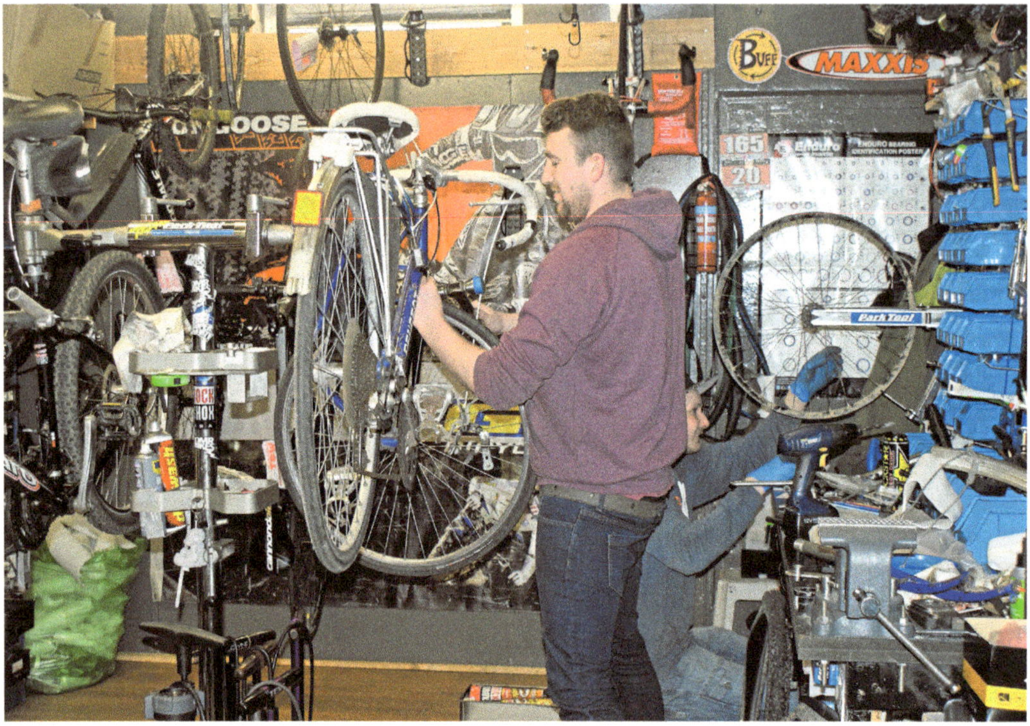

Bike Warehouse, Preston Street.

This ex-Rhodesian explained to me that he had purchased the premises from liquidators and had established a business specialising in vehicle signage and bus restorations and conversions. With all necessary trade skills employed on site, a one-stop solution is provided for customers. In fact, locally trained engineers and apprentices have a combined experience exceeding one hundred years at their fingertips.

Used as a bus depot during 1950s, No. 38 has reverted to its earlier usage. It has in some ways reincarnated into what was once a Victorian horse-drawn vehicle repairers, forge and blacksmiths.

Now operations involve a diverse range of specialist assignments. As well as bespoke bus and coach conversions, other types of public service vehicles can be repaired and altered. There is an enormous choice of trim, upholstery, lighting, decoration, signage and paint livery.

Educational and play vehicles are ordered by schools to promote or enhance their services. A fun category is youth and entertainment mobiles. Buses required by tour and sightseeing companies can be set up for transport of passengers and VIPs. Other lines are training and recruitment vehicles and those used for promotional or exhibition purposes. Also a number of SOS units used in city centres have been prepared, as well as being preferred maintenance repairer for St John Ambulance.

Illustrated overleaf is an ongoing reconstruction of a red London bus. Once undervalued because of their ubiquity following obsolescence, these are presently popular subjects for restoration or conversion into perhaps exhibitors' hospitality stands. Meanwhile this enterprising company's boss is seen contentedly beaming while standing in front of a wonderful example of his creative business – a vivid pink taxi adapted for the needs of a cosmetics client.

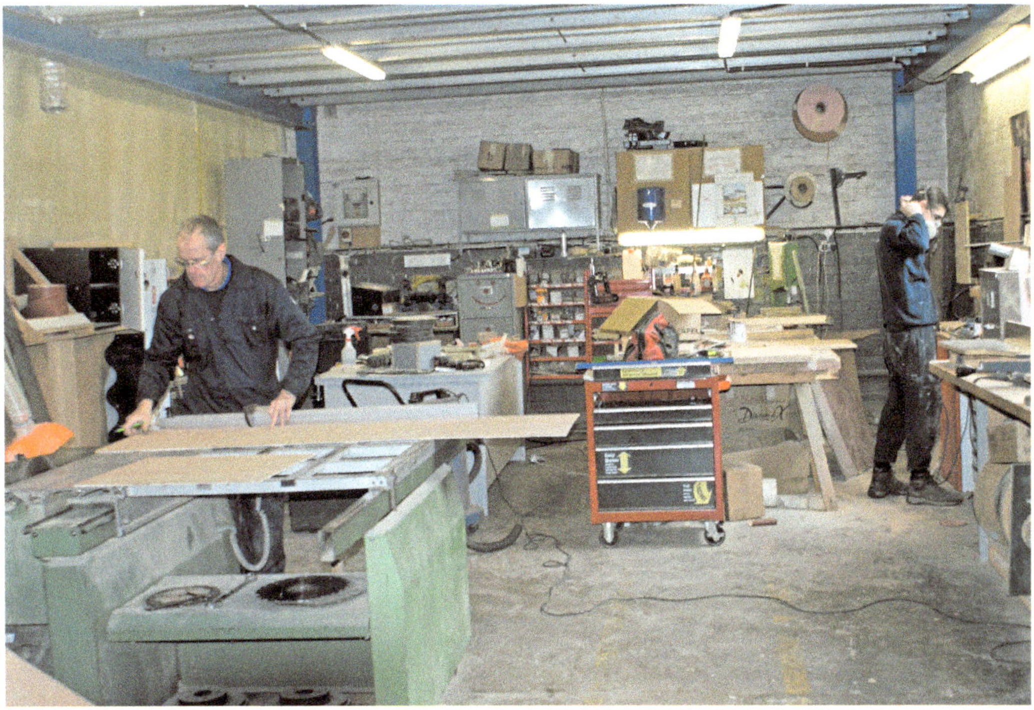

Above: South Eastern Restorations, Preston Street – carpenters workshop.

Right: Conversion work on a London bus.

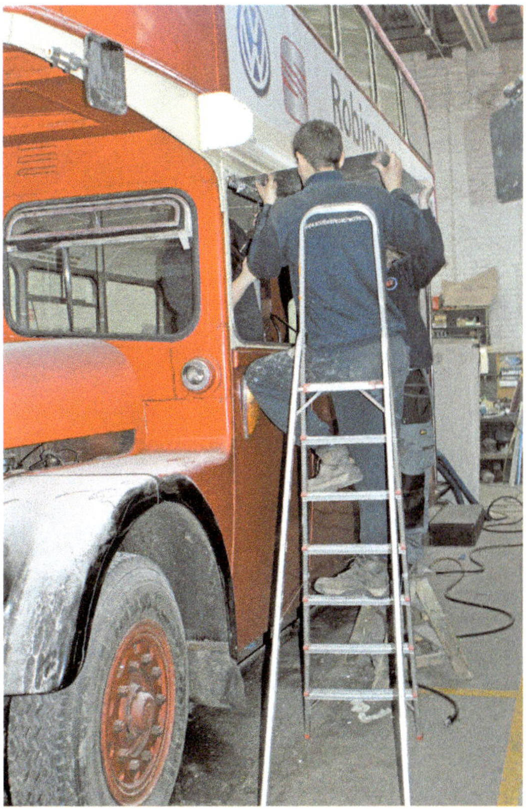

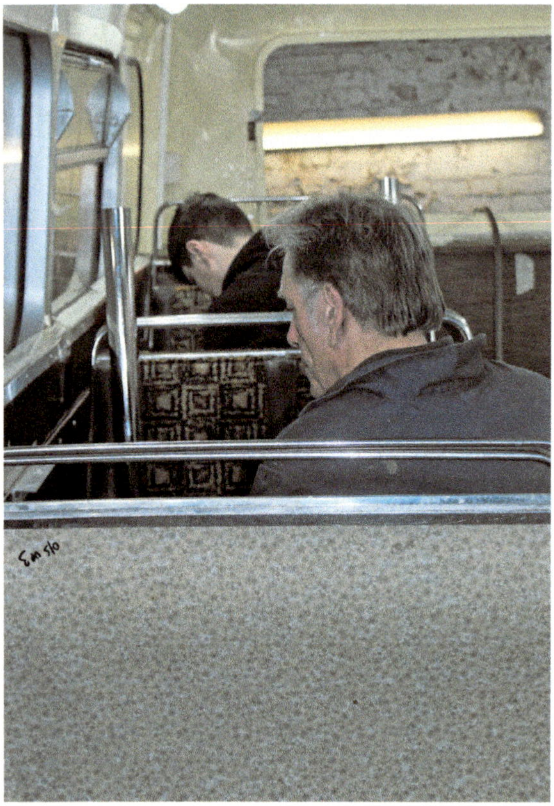

Left: Interior seating adaptations.

Below: Major-domo of South Eastern Restorations, Christopher Bichard Esq.

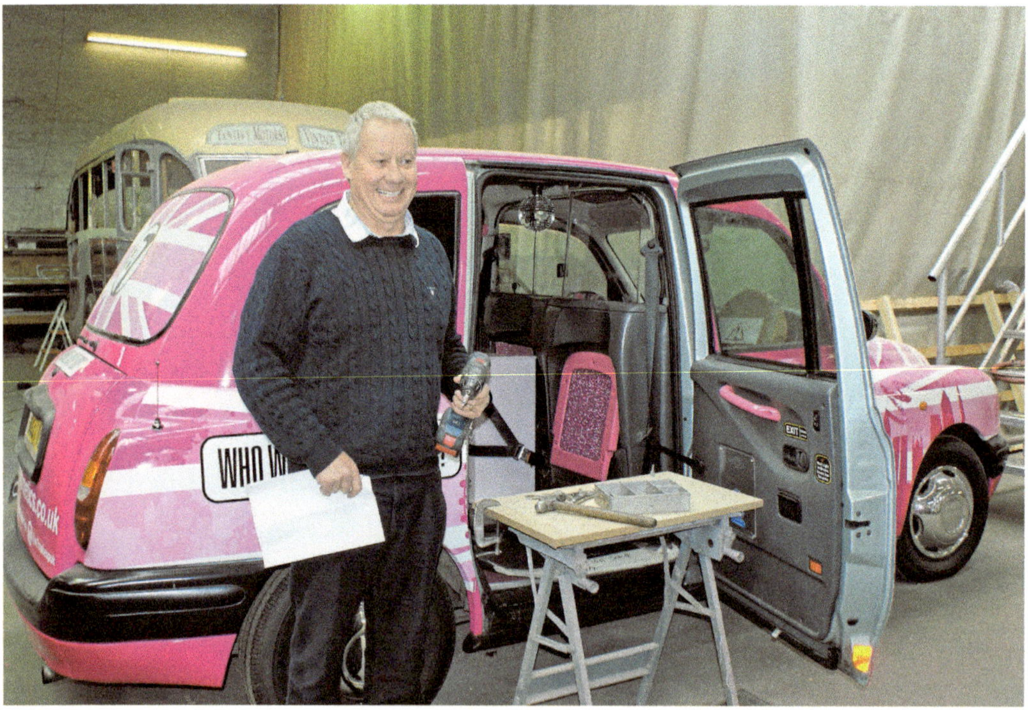

GIST DISTRIBUTION

Gist Distribution at Oare Road have been major employers in the town for over half a century. Their core contract is with Marks & Spencer. High volumes of this retailer's goods constantly arrive from suppliers. These are then sorted into store destinations by order pickers and reloaded onto large articulated lorries. They then drive off to towns dotted around the south-east of England. As volumes have grown, warehouse expansion, by this efficient outfit, has smoothly followed.

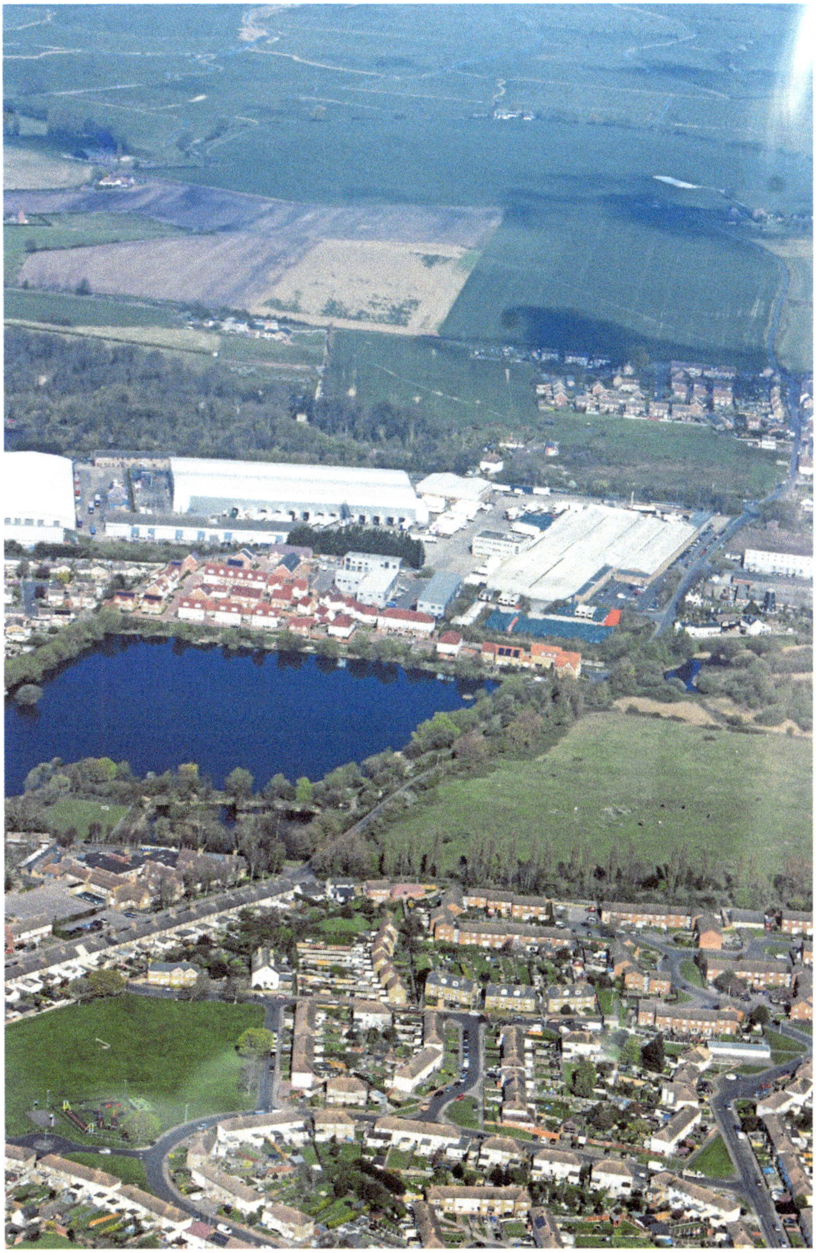

Gist Distribution warehouse.

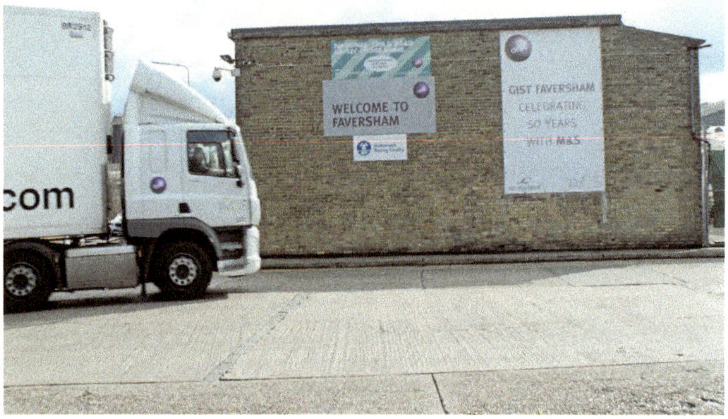

Left: Entrance to Gist Distribution site.

Below: Lorry traffic carrying goods for Marks & Spencer.

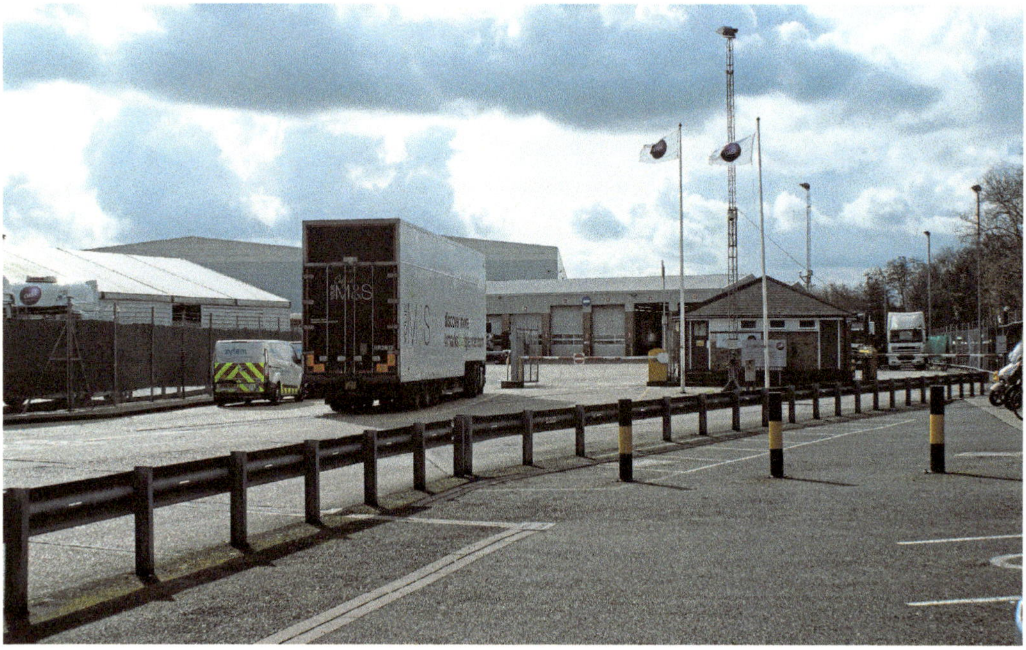

EKS

EKS, which is an acronym for East Kent Storage, can be found close to Gist along Faversham's Western Link road. Being at the heart of a large fruit growing area, this is a good location. The M2 motorway is close with convenient links to London, Dover and the rest of Europe.

An impressive site spread across 8 acres comprises 250,000 square feet of ambient, chilled and controlled atmosphere (CA) storage facilities available under one roof. Fully certified to store organic produce there are 18,000 tonnes of CA and chilled storage available via sixty separate chambers, ranging in size from 150 tonnes to 500+ tonnes.

These good-quality cold-storage facilities are at a premium in the fresh produce industry. Also on offer is nearly 10,000 square feet of modern offices suites available in various sized units.

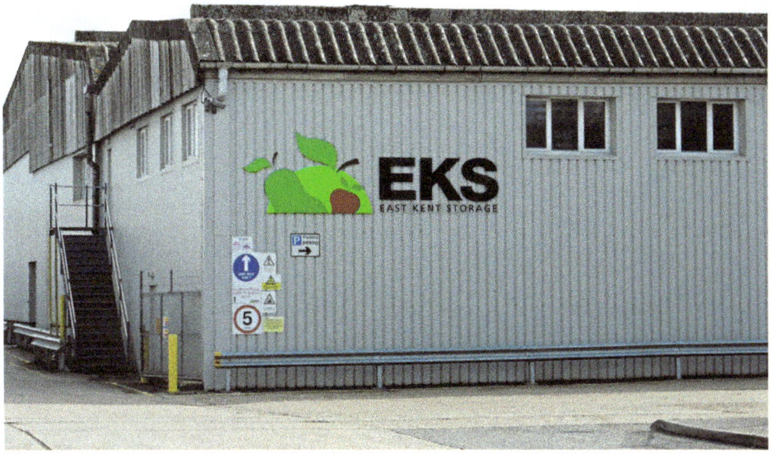

East Kent Storage, Western Link road.

BANKING

Hilton & Rigden Bank was established in 1796 as James Bax, Hilton & Jones or Bax & Co. It underwent many name changes until the Rigden family became involved in 1840. As mentioned previously, this family of considerable substance also had brewery interests. An encashed banknote is shown below, while a picture of gentlemen invited to celebrate Mr Charles Rigden's marriage in 1914 is displayed overleaf.

If one carefully examines the red-brick facade of National Westminster Bank in Market Square, the initials HR can be observed in the masonry. They serve as a small, but permanent, reminder of the once great contribution these people made to the prosperity of Faversham.

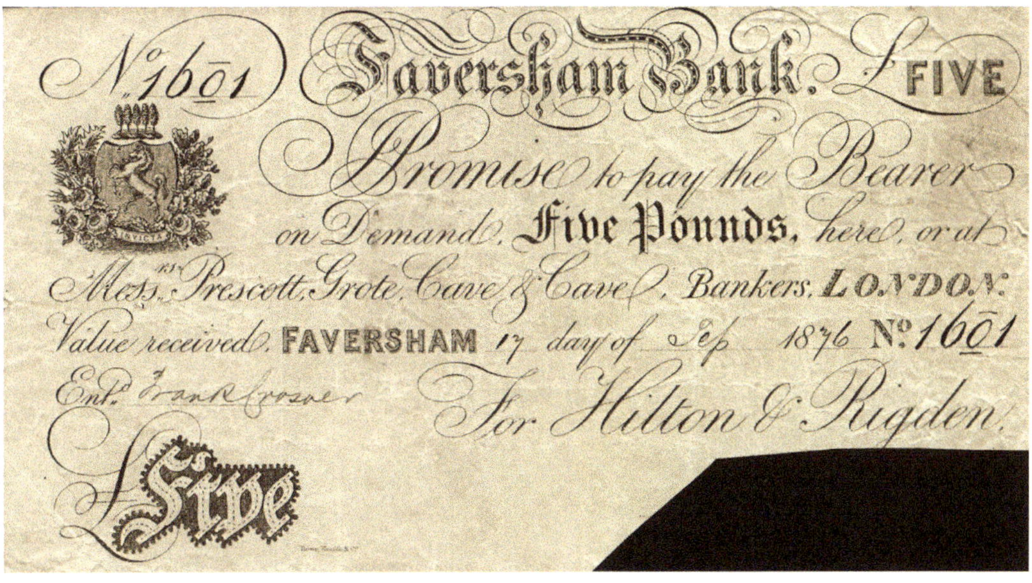

Victorian era white 'fiver' of Faversham Bank.

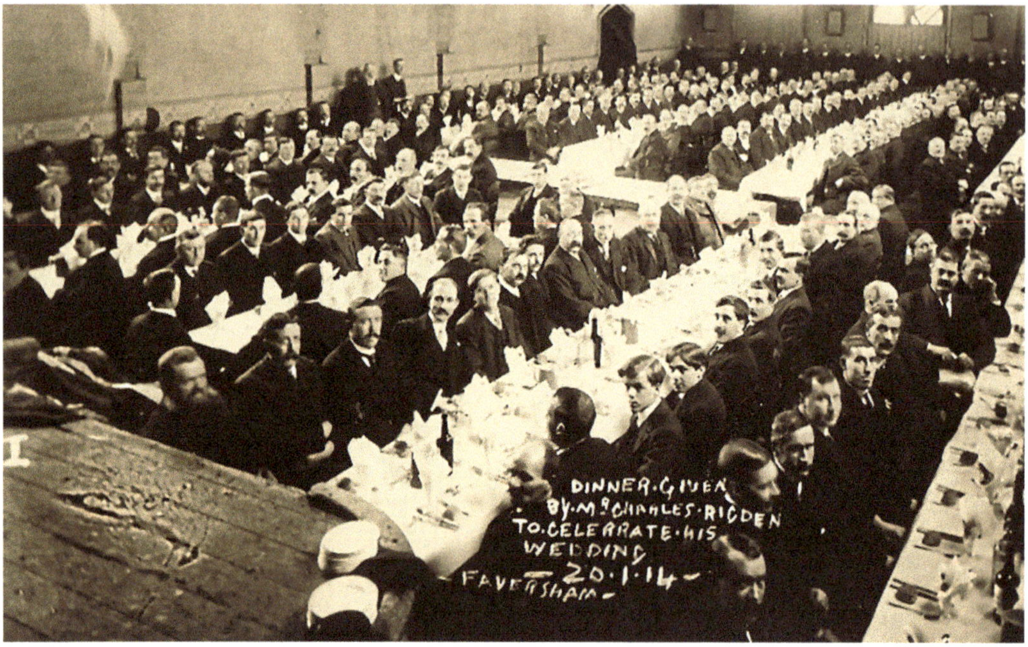

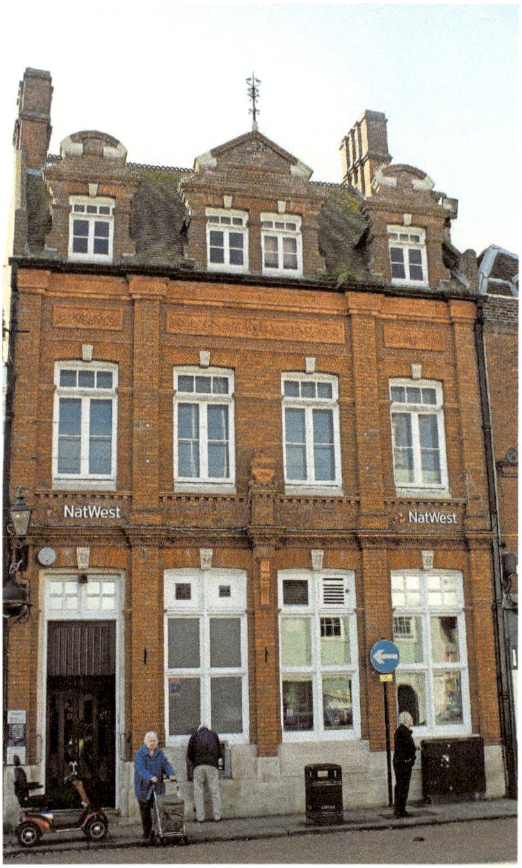

Above: Wedding celebratory meal for brewer Rigden.

Left: National Westminster Bank, Market Square.

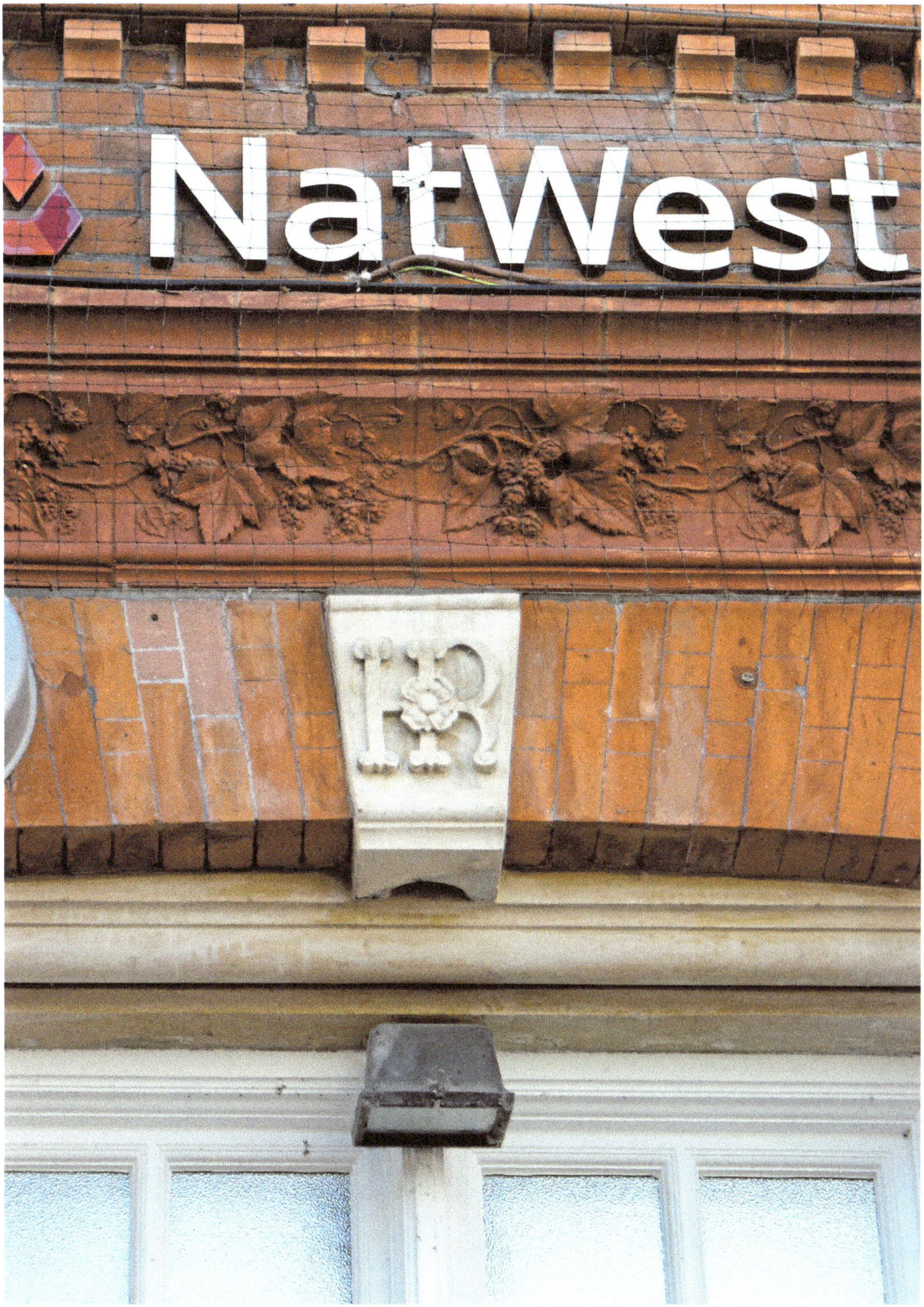

Rigden's initials and motive of hops in brick frieze referencing his other main business interest – brewing.

POLICE

The history of Police in Faversham goes back to a Pavement Act of 1789. Previous to this 'Warders' were in charge of law and order. By 1876 it is recorded that the town's force was led by a head constable (what is now equivalent to an inspector), a sergeant and six constables. The borough force was amalgamated with Kent County Constabulary in 1889. Special (volunteer) constables were recruited from time to time and on an ad hoc basis when there seemed to be a risk of civil disturbance.

The Kent Police Museum is located at Faversham police station. Its vision is to deliver a modern, inspiring and interactive museum that captures the past, present and future of Kent Police. Moreover, they make sure the artefacts on show are safely preserved for future generations to enjoy.

At present police work is supported and overseen by the Police & Crime Commission for Kent. Other criminal justice agencies and partners also help to reduce crime and deliver a first-class service. Methods have changed enormously, however, from the old images overleaf of Bobbies on point duty to squad cars of today – with flashing blue lights – racing to emergency incidents.

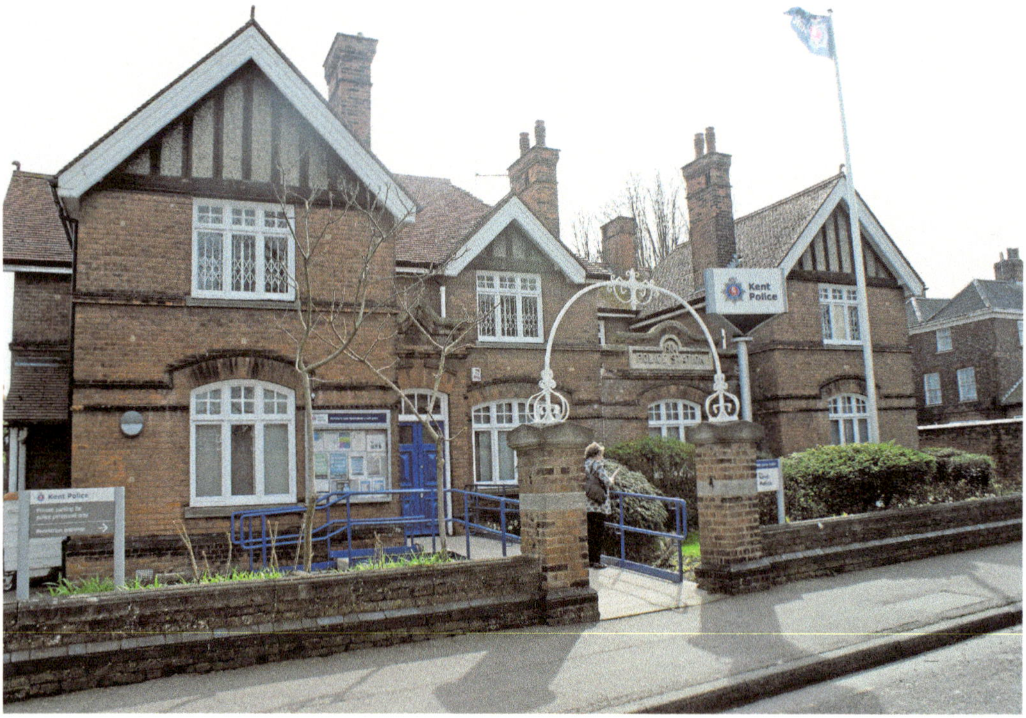

Faversham's previous police station – now a museum.

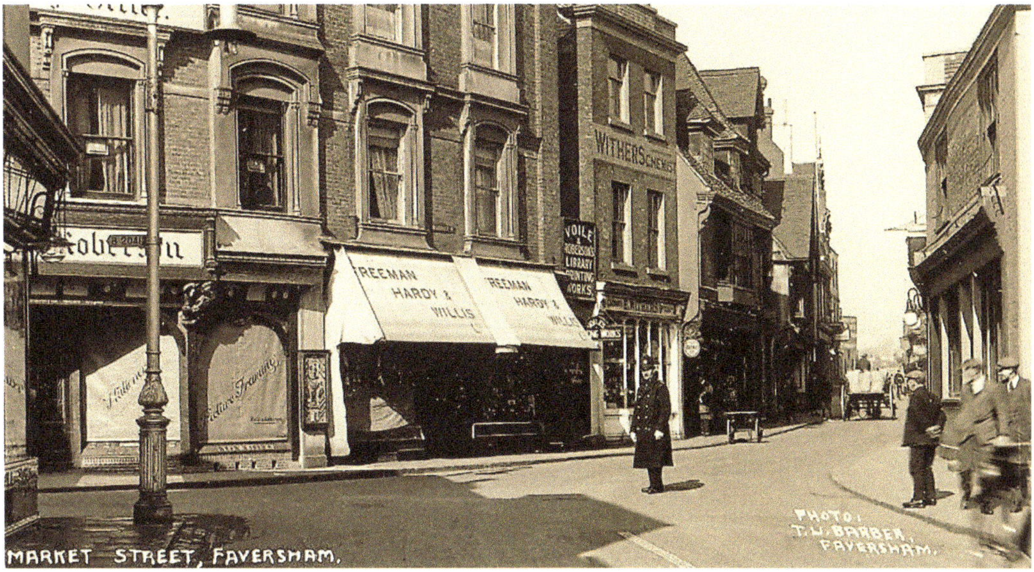

Bobby on point duty at the bottom of Preston Street.

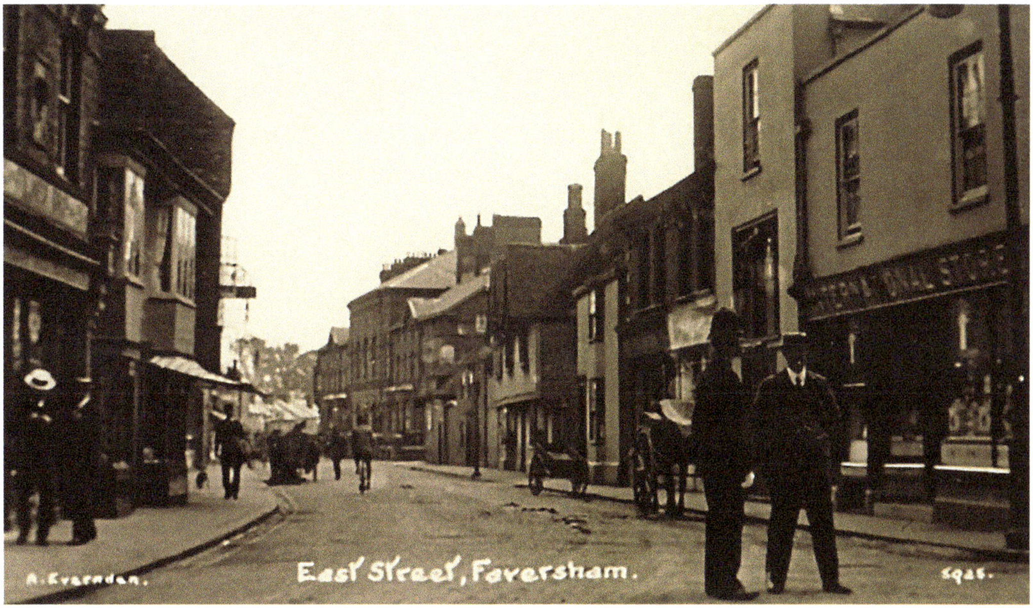

Early tewentieth-century scene of constable in East Street.

FIRE STATION

Faversham Fire Station is based at Beaumont Davy Close south of the A2 road. Before 1939 it was a small building in the middle of town. Operationally this central location was vitally important as response times must have been severely hampered by the time taken to prepare horses and pumps. The gleaming new appliance below was photographed while out on duty. While overleaf is the old fire station and its commemorative plaque.

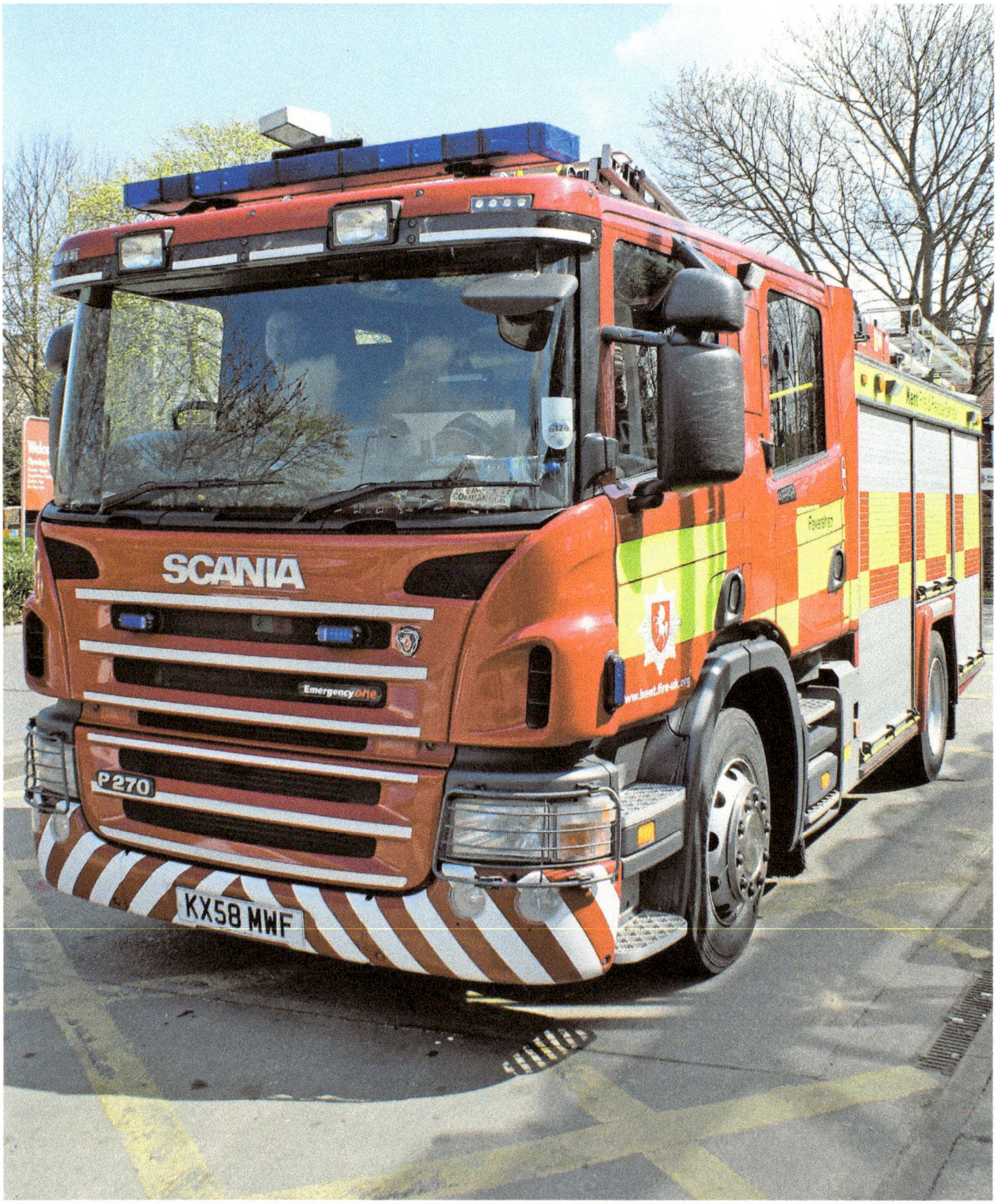

Faversham fire engine.

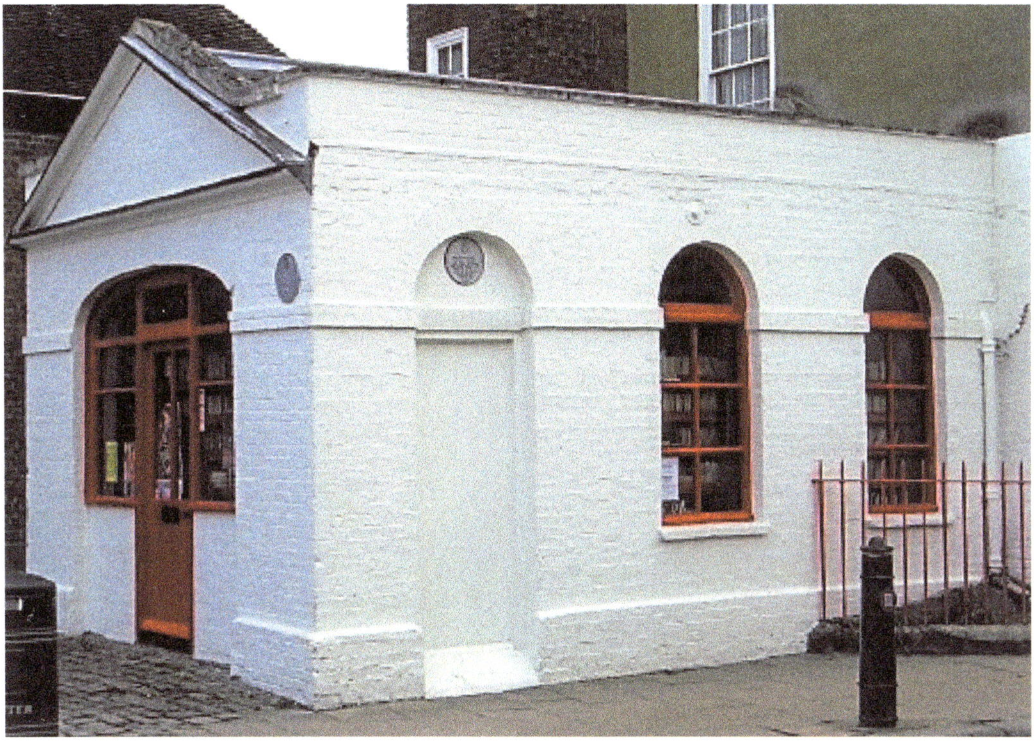

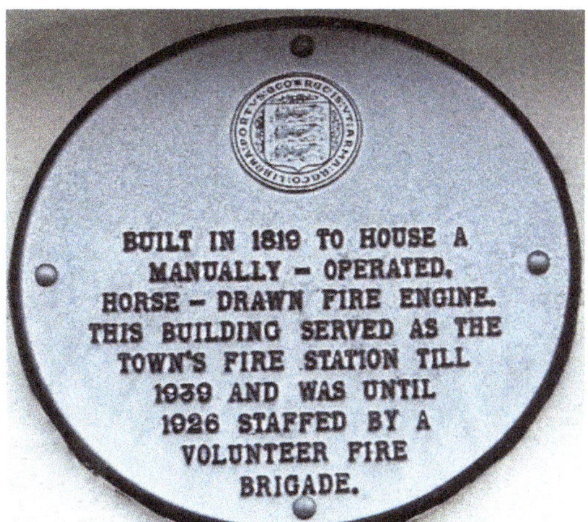

Above: Shelter for horse-drawn fire pump.

Right: Plaque affixed to old fire station in Court Street.

FISHING

Few people are currently employed in commercial fishing along the Swale as this lone boat at work below testifies. In 1836, however, the town had 250 fishermen mainly harvesting oysters. Roman invaders loved them and throughout history they were considered a popular staple food. The company and Fraternity of Free Fishermen of Faversham is claimed to be the oldest corporation as it was set up by at least 1189. There were vast exports to Holland in the eighteenth century, but sadly pollution from sewerage virtually curtailed this industry in around 1900.

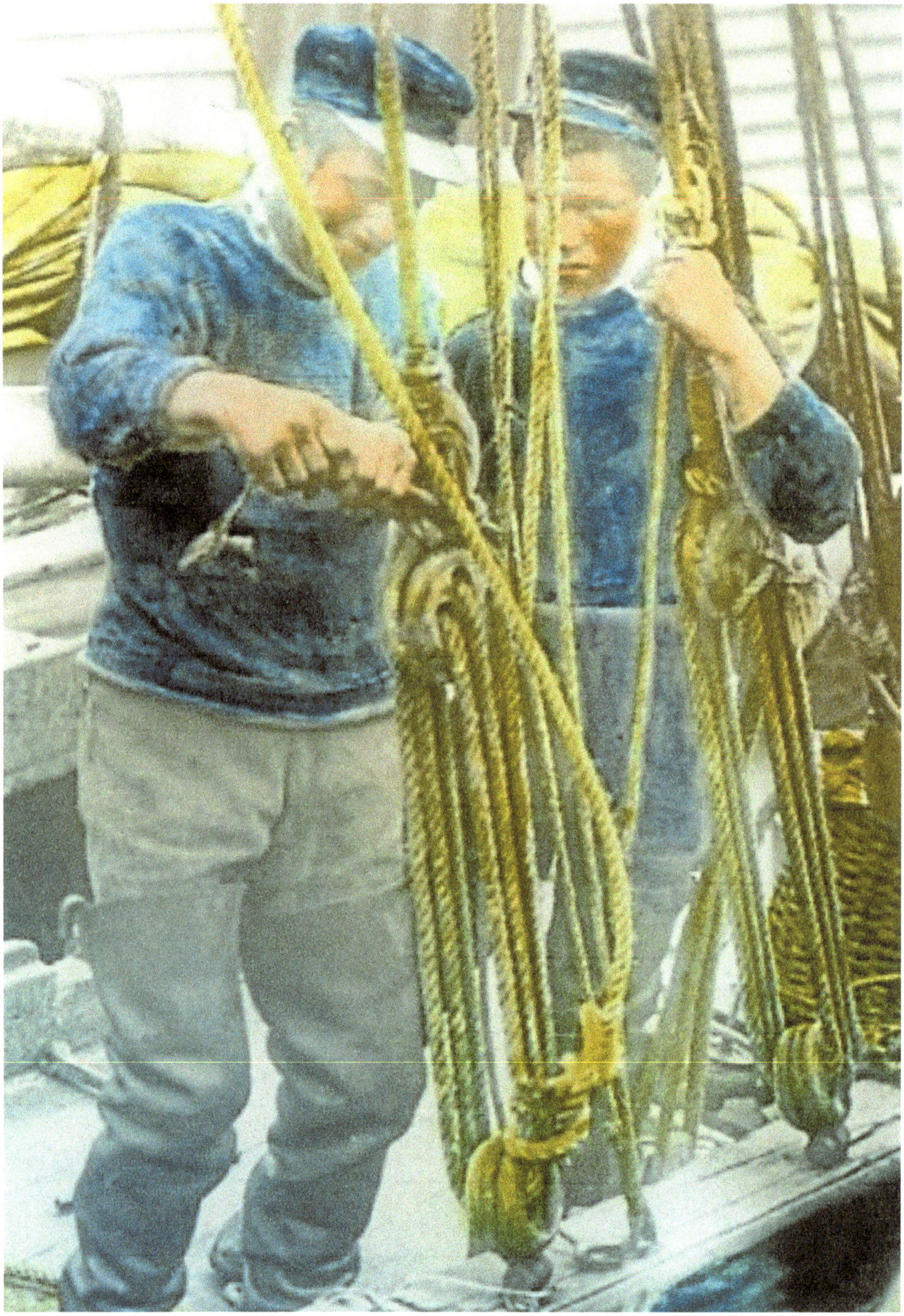

Faversham's skilled mariners of pastimes.

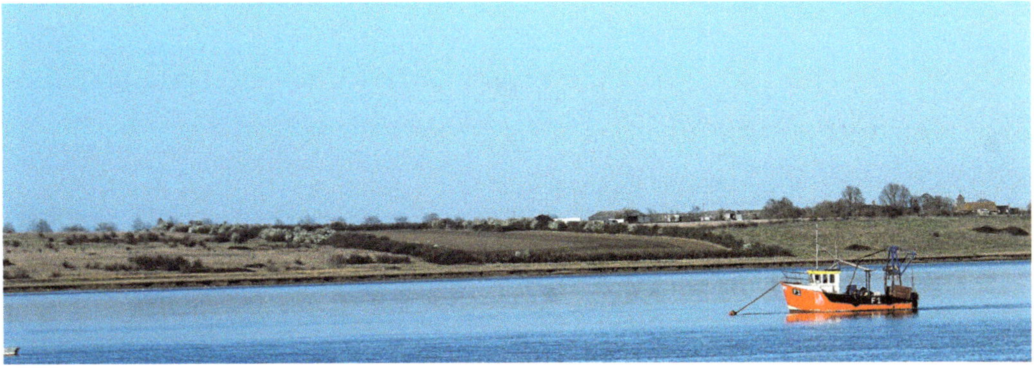

Swale at Harty with a lone fishing boat.

IVOREX PLAQUES

Ivorex Plaques were made in Faversham at No. 83 Abbey Street between 1899 and 1965 by B. Osborne Co., founded by Arthur Osborne, the inspired sculptor of incredible art that he named Ivorex. Collectors have counted over 850 different types that were manufactured. Peak output reached 45,000 per year when fifty operatives were engaged in this work. The process started with formation of a mould. Finishing jobs were painting and lastly waxing.

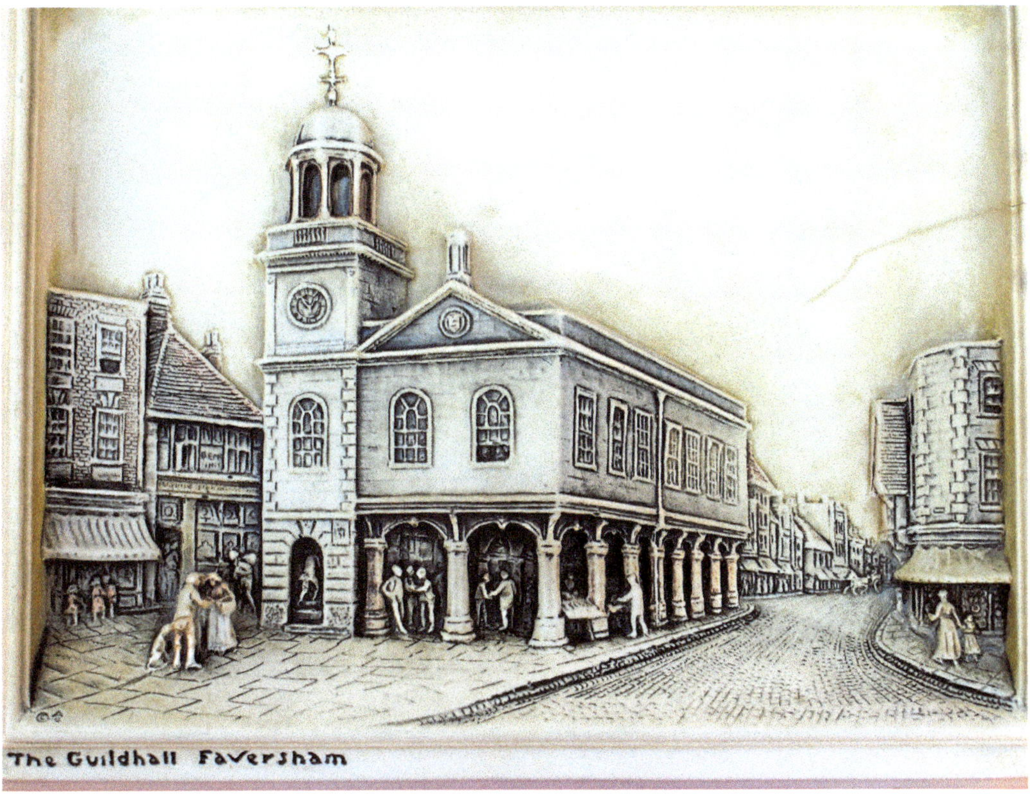

Ivorex/Osborne of Faversham's Guild Hall.

Sales reached most continents of the world – often bought as tourist items as they frequently depicted scenes from postcards. Voile & Roberson (booksellers), who used to have a shop at the bottom of Preston Street, stamped some of the 'Osbornes' in this author's possession. Rare examples today can fetch up to £50, although originally they retailed at prices such as 6*s* 6*d* (32p).

RELIGION

The work of God is personified in Faversham by Revd Sharron Ireland and her colleagues including Revd Simon Rowlands, the vicar of this parish church. They preach to a regular Sunday congregation of sometimes three figures.

As a historic monument this church's distinctive tower is a familiar beacon on the skyline above peg-tiled rooftops. Within its ancient hallowed walls there are memorials to King Stephen and his wife Queen Matilda who resided here. Rarely, there is also a masonry column that retains pre-Reformation colourful frescos depicting bible stories.

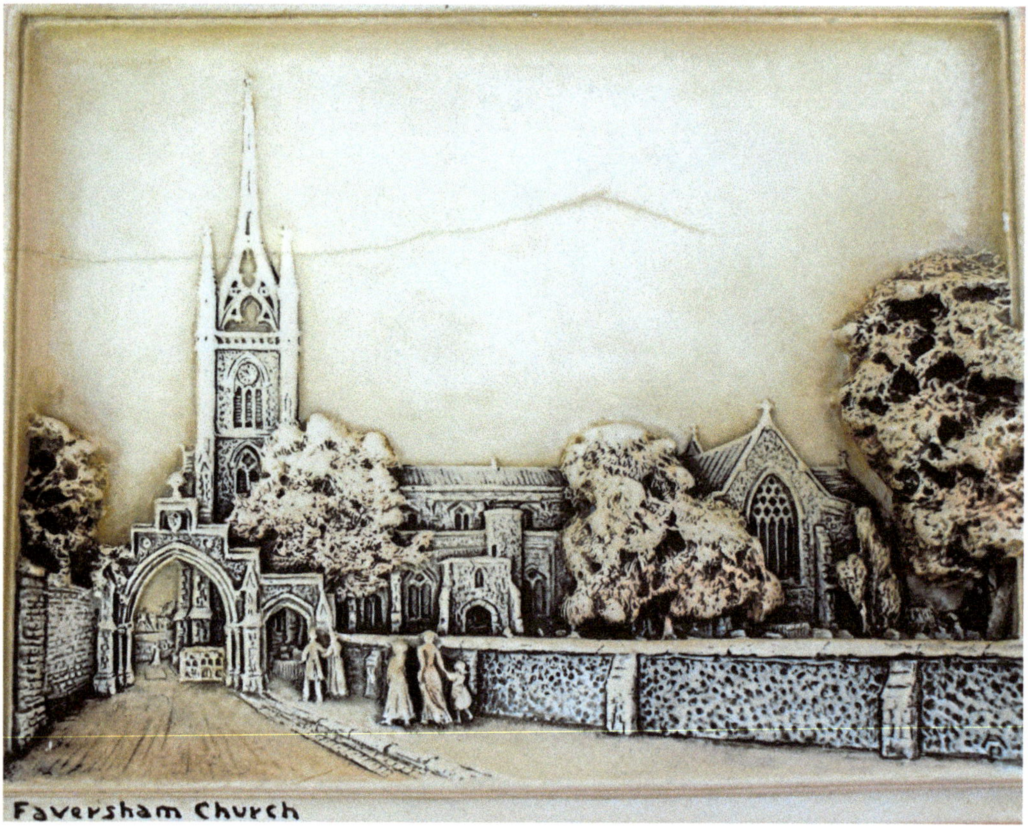

Ivorex of Faversham's distinctive church tower.

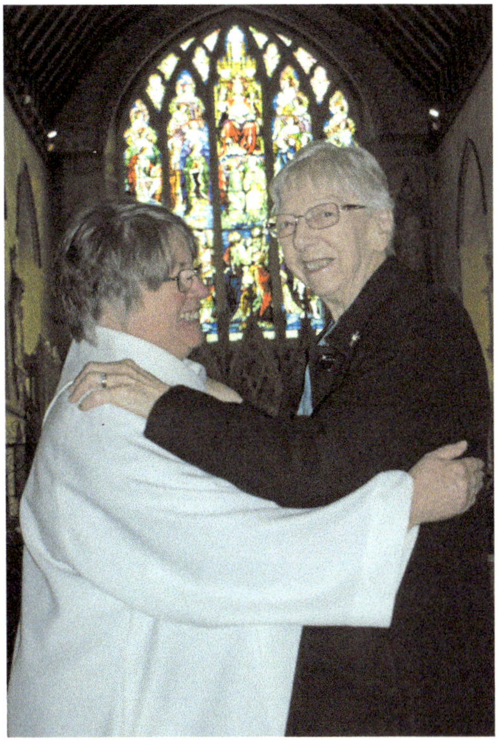

Revd Sharon Ireland embraces a member of her congregation.

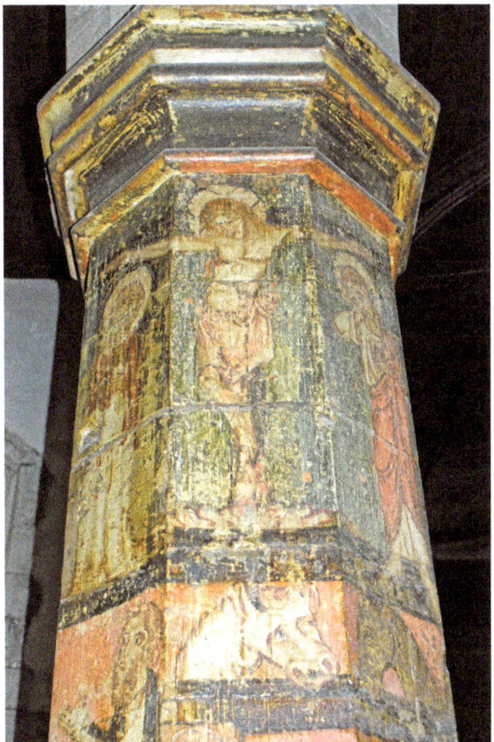

Frescos on Faversham Church column.

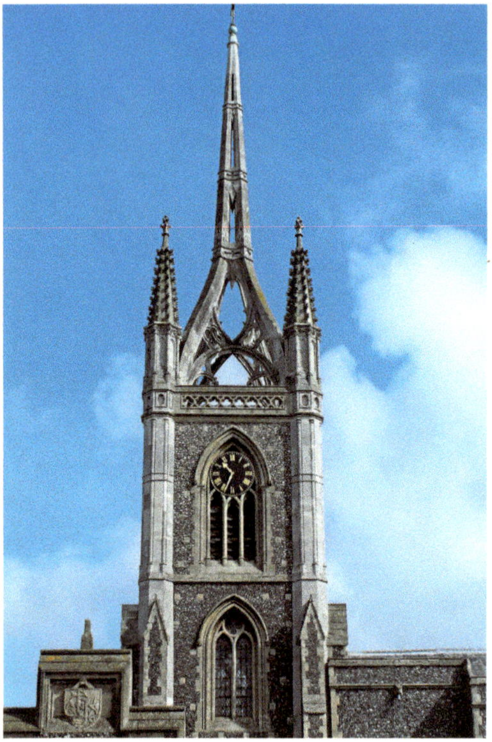

Landmark pinnacle pricking Faversham's skyline.

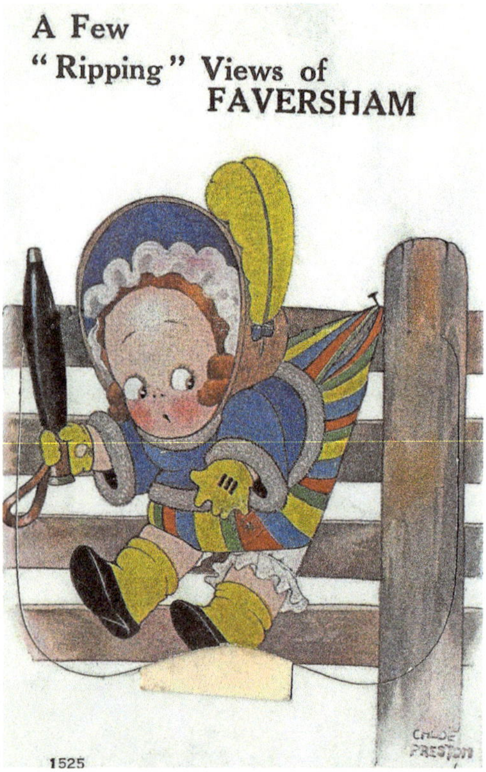

Comic pull-out postcard containing concertina views.